The Illustrated Lives of the

Puccini

Peter Southwell-Sander

OMNIBUS PRESS

To John, with gratitude for the many opera performances we have shared.

Cover design and art direction by Studio Twenty, London
Cover photography by Julian Hawkins

Order No. OP46507
ISBN 0.7119.2754.5

Exclusive Distributors:
Book Sales Limited,
8/9 Frith Street,
London W1V 5TZ, England

Music Sales Corporation
257 Park Avenue South
New York, NY10010, USA

Music Sales Pty Ltd.,
120 Rothschild Avenue,
Rosebery, NSW 2018, Australia

To the Music Trade only:
Music Sales Limited,
8/9 Frith Street,
London WIV 5TZ, England

Design and typesetting by DMC Design

Printed and bound in the United Kingdom by
Staples Printers Limited, Rochester, Kent

A catalogue record for this book is available from the British Library

Contents

Foreword

Opera is being appreciated by larger and larger audiences, and the music of Giacomo Puccini has played an important part in this. It was a televised performance of *La bohème* from the Metropolitan Opera in New York in 1977, in which I and Renata Scotto sang Rodolfo and Mimi, that was the first of my many televised broadcasts and concerts to audiences in venues like Madison Square Garden in New York or London's Hyde Park, which have allowed me to play my part in bringing opera to a wider audience. It has been a great pleasure to me that my recording of 'Nessun dorma' from Puccini's *Turandot,* used as the theme tune for the 1990 Football World Cup in Italy, has encouraged many thousands of people, who had not appreciated opera before, to listen to recordings, and come to concerts and performances of opera.

Puccini has a special place in my heart, because I made my professional début as Rodolfo in *La bohème* on 29 April 1961 in the Teatro Municipale in Reggio Emilia. As most of us were débutante singers, we spent six weeks living in a Bohemian hotel, studying Mürger's *Scènes de la vie de bohème* and looking at how Puccini and his librettists had adapted it. By doing this, we came to know Puccini's intentions better and so gained a deeper understanding of *La bohème.* It has always been very important for me to study the background to the operas and the parts I perform. It makes a great difference to how I interpret a rôle.

As a result of reading more about Puccini the man and the operas he composed, I hope that your enjoyment of the drama and the music of his operas will become even greater.

Luciano Pavarotti

Giacomo Puccini.

Chapter 1

Heir to a Tradition

Almighty God touched me with His little finger and said: 'Write for the theatre – mind, only for the theatre.' (Puccini in an undated letter to Giuseppe Adami, Spring 1920.)

'Bohème, Tosca and *Madama Butterfly*...are operas that speak above all to the emotions of the public, and speak in a voice that is original, moving, penetrating and sincere.' Those words of Giulio Gatti-Casazza, former general manager of the New York Metropolitan Opera and before that of La Scala, Milan, are part of a tribute he gave shortly after the composer's death. They express the response of generations of audiences, who have encountered moments in Puccini operas where music and drama combine to stir deeply-seated emotions, often touching and illuminating episodes and moments in their own lives.

Such music-lovers are bemused when they hear of the denigration of the same operas by professional musicians. Joseph Kerman's dismissal of *Tosca* as 'that shoddy little shocker' is well-known. Stravinsky contemptuously referred to *La fanciulla del West* as 'a remarkably up-to-date TV horse opera', while Benjamin Britten remarked that he was 'sickened by the cheapness and emptiness' of Puccini's music. Even in Puccini's lifetime critics could be equally negative. In a book on Puccini in 1912, Fausto Torrefranca wrote: 'He seems to me the composer who personifies with greatest completeness the decadence of today's Italian music, and who represents its cynical commercialism, its lamentable impotence, its celebration of the international vogue.' Yet Puccini operas remain among the most performed and popular in the operatic repertoire the world over.

This ability to command enormous popular success, not only in his own time but in the present day, in stark contrast to the disparagement of his music by critical opinion, has a parallel in his early life. Born into a family of composers, he

Puccini's great-great grandfather, Giacomo Puccini (1712-81). *(left)*

Antonio Benedetto Maria Puccini, Giacomo's great-grandfather. *(below)*

was expected to follow the provincial tradition of his ancestors. Yet he was soon irritated by his conventional musical education and the life mapped out for him by the musical establishment, adopting a life-style that was both flamboyant and adventurous with its share of personal torment and sorrow. By combining these elements of high spirits and ostentation with tragedy, Puccini was to create some enormously successful musical dramas that spoke directly to the experience of his public. In spite of breaking away from some aspects of his family tradition, his roots remained important to him throughout his life. He never moved far from the town of his birth, and only a month before his death paid a long-promised visit to the tiny village of Celle in the Apuan Alps, the home of his forefathers. A touching photograph of the occasion shows the internationally-acclaimed composer, swaggeringly confident, surrounded by a group of local worthies.

Puccini at Celle, a month before his death in October 1924.

It was from this remote hamlet that his great-great-great

10

The Cathedral of
San Martino, Lucca.

grandfather had moved south to Lucca, the mediaeval capital of Tuscany, once one of the important city-states of central Italy. From him stretch a line of organist/composers, who contributed significantly to Lucca's musical tradition of church music and that unique Lucchese musical form, the *tasche*, a kind of early oratorio. Performed on the election of a new government at the *Festa delle tasche* (the Feast of the Pouches – the receptacles for voting papers), these works drew a total of 32 contributions from three of Puccini's forebears to add to those of that other celebrated local composer, Luigi

11

Boccherini. When Napoleon abolished the Republic of Lucca in 1799 these entertainments ceased. A similar fate befell another speciality of the city, the *mottetone*, composed for the Feast of the Holy Cross. All four of Puccini's composer forebears wrote in this genre. However, as these cantatas became increasingly secular in nature, Pope Pius X eventually banned them in 1904.

Only the Bachs number more generations of composers than the Puccinis. Nothing is known of the Puccini who moved from Celle to Lucca, but his son Giacomo (1712-81), after studying at Bologna – probably under the great music teacher and scholar, Padre Martini, became conductor of Lucca's Cappella Palatina as well as organist and choirmaster of the Cathedral of San Martino. Antonio (1747-1832), son of Giacomo, also studied at Bologna and was there when the 14-year-old Mozart, having been assessed and acclaimed by Padre Martini, was received into the renowned Accademia dei Filarmonici, an honour also accorded to Antonio himself. He succeeded his father in both his posts at Lucca, composing not only religious and secular works, but also operas.

In 1805, Napoleon, as part of his policy of surrounding the empire with vassal states ruled by his relatives, installed his eldest sister Elisa Baciochi as Princess of the Principality of Lucca and Piombino, and, four years later, as Grand Duchess of Tuscany. As a result, Antonio lost his job as director of the Cappella Palatina when it was dissolved during her initial sweeping reforms. These included a major re-building programme during which an entire mediaeval quarter was demolished to create an open space in front of the Ducal Palace, which she named Piazza Napoleone. She also commissioned the architect Lorenzo Nottolino to design an elliptical 'square' of houses following the line of the foundations of the second-century Roman amphitheatre. Although the Princess's musical reforms were to the disadvantage of Antonio Puccini, his son Domenico (1771-1815) was appointed musical director of her personal orchestra, the Cappella da Camera. Paganini was invited to conduct it in 1809 as well as several operas at court; he stayed in a house which still bears the inscription: 'Love and Poverty tormented his genius but the city rendered the wings of glory to his mysterious violin.' Domenico Puccini, who studied under the operatic composer Paisiello, wrote a successful *opera seria*, *Il trionfo di Quinto Fabio*, and several comic operas, some of which were performed by aristocratic amateurs at private performances. He died rather suddenly, amidst rumours that, for upholding liberal ideas, he had been given a cup of poisoned sherbet at an

Austrian nobleman's party. In 1814, the Congress of Vienna
put Tuscany under the control of the Bourbons of Parma, first
in the person of Marie Louise and then her son Carlo
Ludovico, both of whom continued to support and encourage
music in Lucca. An obvious visible sign of this change is a
statue of Marie Louise erected in place of a planned monument
to Napoleon in the Piazza that bears his name.

One of Domenico Puccini's four children, Michele (born in
1813), studied at Bologna and then Naples, where he was
taught by both Donizetti and Mercadante, who were, with
Rossini and Bellini, the most important Italian opera
composers in the period before Verdi. Though Gaetano
Donizetti (1797-1848) wrote 65 operas in a wide range of
styles, he is best-known for his comic operas such as *L'elisir
d'amore* and *Don Pasquale*; an irony indeed, for his personal life
was full of tragedy. Two of his children were stillborn, while
the third only survived for a few days. His parents died within a
few weeks of each other to be closely followed by his young
wife in a cholera epidemic. Donizetti himself contracted

13

Puccini's father Michele.

cerebrospinal syphilis, from which he died after a harrowing illness, paralysed and hardly able to speak. Michele's other teacher, Giuseppe Mercadante (1795-1870), was also a prolific opera composer. Though not of the stature of Rossini, Bellini or Donizetti, he had a considerable influence on Verdi, who much admired him.

Following family tradition, Michele returned to Lucca to become organist and choirmaster at the Cathedral of San Martino, and was respected as a teacher and composer of church and secular music, including two operas that enjoyed modest success. He also became director of the Conservatoire, later known as the Istituto Musicale Pacini after its first director, the opera composer Giovanni Pacini (1796-1867). It had been founded by Carlo Ludovico, who merged all the town's music schools together. In 1943, in recognition of the bicentenary of the birth of another famous Lucchese composer, it was re-named the Istituto Musicale Luigi Boccherini. Michele Puccini married the sister of a former pupil, Albina Magi, who was 18 years his junior. On 23 January 1864, Michele died, leaving her with six children and a seventh due. The fifth child had been born, according to his birth certificate on 22 December 1858 (though he always insisted his birthday was 23 December). As the first son, he was duly named after his composer forebears, Giacomo Antonio Domenico Michele Secondo Maria Puccini.

There was clearly a weighty expectation that Giacomo should become a musician. In an oration at Michele's funeral, Pacini called the five-year-old boy 'the sole survivor of and heir to that glory which his ancestors have earned in the harmonious Art and which perhaps one day it will be in his power to revive'. Albina's brother, Fortunato Magi, was appointed to succeed Michele only on condition that he would 'hand over the post of Organist and Maestro di Cappella to Signor Giacomo, son of the aforementioned defunct master, as soon as the said Signor Giacomo be able to discharge such duties'. Lucca's faith in the Puccini family tradition was unshakeable. In dwelling on the richness of Puccini's musical inheritance, both his contemporaries and music historians since have tended to overlook the willpower, character and creative brilliance that enabled Puccini to free himself from the clutches of the narrow, provincial musical tradition into which he was born.

Giacomo's home town of Lucca in north-west Tuscany is separated by Mount Pisano to the south from the coastal plain created by the River Arno flowing through Florence and Pisa to the sea. To the north are the Apennines and the Apuan Alps. Originally settled by the Estruscans, it became a Roman

14

town in 180 BC. Much fought over because of its importance as a military staging post it was ruled by others, including the Lombards, until it eventually became an independent city state in 1115. The twelfth and thirteenth centuries saw its heyday as a commercial centre with its wealth derived mainly from the weaving and export of its famous silks. In contrast to Gothic Siena and Renaissance Florence, Lucca is principally Romanesque. Many of the churches and the new brick houses of that time were built with bell-towers, leaving the visitor with a striking impression of campaniles and towers rising above the red-tiled roofs.

After its golden age, weakened by civil wars, Lucca was once more dominated by outsiders, culminating in the harsh rule of Pisa for the first 30 years of the fifteenth century, from which it

View of Lucca, Tuscany.

only regained its independence under Charles V, subsequently existing peacefully under a Council of Elders for the next four centuries. Although it never had to withstand a siege, a set of magnificent sixteenth-century walls and ramparts was built in the shape of a polygon round the enlarged city. Later this was converted into a tree-lined promenade, though sadly the Austrians subsequently removed the 124 ancient cannon from the bastions. Lucca had its share of wealthy families as the 40 or so surviving *palazzi* testify. Some, like the notable Palazzo Guingi with oak trees growing on top of its tower, date back to the fourteenth century, but during the sixteenth and seventeenth centuries others like the Palazzo Mansi were built with less emphasis on external decoration, seemingly in keeping with the quiet, isolated nature of the town. Such restraint was not demonstrated inside however, where, more often than not, the visitor was overwhelmed by the golds and reds of the baroque – with stucco, carving, paintings and furniture complementing the Lucchese silk hangings and tapestries. The great families of Lucca, the Mansi and Torrigiani for example, tried to rival the Medici of Florence. They enlarged their villas outside the town, decorating them with statues, porticoes, external staircases and loggias, and surrounding them with spacious parks containing fountains, pools, more statues and carefully-created panoramic vistas.

The house in which Puccini was brought up was in stark contrast to such opulence. His widowed mother, Albina, struggled to bring up her large family in their first-floor apartment in the unprepossessing three-storeyed house at 30 Via di Poggio, now a Puccini museum. She enlisted her brother, Fortunato, to teach 'Giacomino' to sing and play the organ. We know the boy was lazy – receiving consistently bad school reports. Whenever possible he would escape with his friends and his younger brother, Michele – born three months after his father's death – to play on the mediaeval town walls or hunt birds in the fields beyond. It soon became clear that the short-tempered uncle was making little headway with his nephew's musical education. It is said that he used to kick Giacomo on the shin when he sang a wrong note – which apparently accounted for the fact that ever after Puccini's leg twitched nervously whenever he heard someone singing out of tune. Albina, therefore, arranged to transfer him in 1874 to another of her husband's former pupils, Carlo Angeloni, at the Pacini Institute. Previously, at the age of ten, he had become a choirboy in the Cathedral of San Martino, as well as the church of San Michele, where, four years later, he began to play the organ.

Puccini also played the piano in taverns to earn money to

Puccini's mother Albina.

30 Via di Poggio, Lucca, where Puccini was born and where he spent most of his childhood.

support his family and, it was rumoured, in houses of ill repute. There are many tales that attempt to fill in our sketchy knowledge of his adolescence, which, as Italians would say, *se non è vera, è ben trovata* (even if they're not true, they're good stories). He had begun to smoke at an early age, and, to pay for

Giuseppi Verdi (1813-1901), whose opera *Aida* was so admired by the young Puccini.

cigarettes or the local short cigars, *toscanos*, it is said that he and some friends stole organ pipes to sell as scrap metal. His ingenuity was then stretched to improvise on the organ avoiding the missing pipes. His improvisations – an important element in the organist's art – were sometimes criticised for their introduction of folk tunes and snatches of opera. 'You're trying to outdo the theatre', was the tart comment of Iginia, his elder sister shortly to become an Augustinian nun. His first formal organ compositions were written when he was 16 for his first pupil.

Lucca was fortunate in having three venues where operas were performed, but these were mainly local productions with inferior singers. Angeloni introduced his pupil to opera beyond such narrow confines, initially through the scores of Verdi's three great middle-period operas *Rigoletto*, *La traviata* and *Il trovatore*, all first performed only a few years before Puccini's birth. Giuseppe Verdi (1813-1901), succeeding Rossini, Bellini and Donizetti, had dominated and transformed Italian opera. His was a towering genius that encapsulated in his operas the longing for national and individual freedom that had swept

18

through Italy during the period of the *Risorgimento*, the movement for a united Italy free from Austrian rule. Dealing in large-scale canvasses and grand themes like justice, truth and freedom, Verdi had the rare ability of the truly great artist to explore these within the situations of particular people and places, while at the same time lifting personal misfortune up to the level of tragic heroism. He was now in his sixties, and, though he was to live into the next century and write *Otello* and *Falstaff*, there were those who were already seeking a potential successor. Learning that *Aida* was to be performed for the first time in Pisa on 11 March 1876, Puccini and two friends walked the 20 miles and conned their way into the theatre without tickets. It was an experience that changed his life. He recalled later: 'When I heard *Aida* at Pisa, I felt that a musical window had been opened for me.'

Applying himself with more determination to his studies, Puccini wrote the orchestral *Preludio sinfonico* that year, and the next year a setting of a patriotic poem *I figli d'Italia bella* for a competition. The judges did not award him a prize, commenting that the manuscript was almost indecipherable. His illegible scores were to remain a problem throughout his life. A Motet and Credo of 1878 in honour of Lucca's patron saint San Paolino, to whom is attributed the invention of church bells, were more successful. Two years later, he incorporated them into a Mass for four voices and orchestra. Not published until 1951, it is now know as the *Messa di gloria*. Angeloni thought it 'a little theatrical', and the local newspaper saw in it some 'extremely noble ideas'. An eclectic work by an immature composer, it harks back to Verdi's Requiem of six years earlier, echoing Bellini, Donizetti and even Gounod. Yet there are signs of the Puccini to come. Indeed, he was later to use parts of it in *Edgar* and *Manon Lescaut*, though the fact that the Agnus Dei could be transformed into a song to accompany a lady's toilet says much about Puccini's attitude to sacred music and even to religion itself.

This was his graduation piece for the Istituto Musicale Pacini. His sights were now set on the Milan Conservatoire. His redoubtable mother obtained a scholarship for his first year by a direct appeal to Queen Margherita of Savoy, wife of King Umberto I. When subsequent requests for assistance were turned down by the Lucchese authorities, she persuaded her bachelor uncle, Dr Nicolao Cerù, to support her son in his remaining two years as a student. Cerù wrote a gossip column for a local paper in which, commenting on the Mass of 1880, he had quoted the proverb: *I figli dei gatti prendono i topi*, or, as we might put it, 'He's a chip off the old block.'

Giacomo Puccini in his
student years.

Giacomo found the entrance examination for Milan 'ridicu-
lously easy' and was admitted to study under the professor of
composition Antonio Bazzini (1818-97), a notable violinist
and composer, whose only opera *Turanda* was based on
Gozzi's *Turandot*, the source Puccini would himself turn to 40
years later for his last opera. On 18 December 1880, he wrote
to his mother:

I have made myself this timetable: in the morning I get up at eight-
thirty, and when I have a lesson I go to it. If I have no lesson, I practise the piano a little. I don't need to do much, but I have to practise
a bit. I am going to buy a very good *Method* by Angeleri, the sort of
method from which one can learn a lot by oneself. I go on till ten-
thirty; then I have lunch and go out. At one o'clock I come home and
then work for a couple of hours preparing for Bazzini. From three to
about five I study some classical music at the piano. I'd like to take
out a subscription for scores, but I haven't enough money. At the
moment I am reading the *Mefistofele* of Boito, which a friend of mine,
Favara from Palermo, has lent me. At five I go to my frugal meal
(special emphasis on the frugal!), and I have Milanese broth, which,
to tell the truth, is very good. I have three plates of that, then some
other mess, a bit of Gorgonzola cheese, and half a litre of wine. Then
I light a cigar and go off to my usual walk up and down in the
Galleria. I am there till nine o'clock and come home dead tired. I do
a little counterpoint, but no playing; I am not allowed to play at
night. Then I get into bed and read seven or eight pages of a novel.
And that's my life!

All his letters to his mother betray a preoccupation with
money. The poverty of his early years was to leave its mark on
him, so that, even when he was very rich, he remained conspic-
uously tight-fisted. In his second year, he shared lodgings with
his brother Michele, a cousin, and Pietro Mascagni, later to
achieve fame with *Cavalleria rusticana*. It is uncertain how
much the setting of *La bohème* influenced the memories of
those who later recounted how Puccini would hide in the
wardrobe to avoid creditors or play the piano to cover the noise
of their illegal cooking. During this time he heard as many
operas as possible, including Thomas's *Mignon*, the revised
version of Verdi's *Simon Boccanegra*, Bizet's *Carmen* and
Dejanice by Alfredo Catalani (1854-93). The latter also came
from Lucca and was most kind to his younger fellow-citizen at
the beginning of his career. Catalani was influenced by
German Romanticism, so, as the *verismo* school gained ground
and his own works consequently fell into disfavour, he was to
become sadly hostile to Puccini.

Among the leading exponents of *verismo* (realism, from *vero*

Alfredo Catalini in his 20s.

Entrance of the "Pagliacci"

1st Act

Entrance of the *pagliacci* as shown in *The Illustrated London News* of 27 May 1893.

– true) in Italian literature was Giovanni Verga (1840-1922), who wrote true-to-life stories of his native Sicily, *Vita dei campi* (1880), in which he vividly conveyed the idiomatic speech of Sicilian peasants. His impersonal, objective narrative style, his subjects taken from contemporary life, and his concentration on the lower social classes in the southern regions of Italy were typical characteristics of the writings of the *veristi*. The clown, Tonio, in the Prologue to Leoncavallo's one-act opera *Pagliacci* (1832), gives a neat description of *verismo* by announcing to the audience that 'the author will take a slice of life (*uno squarcio di vita*) with its laughter and sorrow'. Such operas, in their search for realism, followed the lead of the '*scene popolari*' of Verga and others by depicting very ordinary people and the everyday events of their lives, into which heightened emotion and even violence could erupt. The one-act form proved ideal for this; *Cavalleria rusticana* (based on a Verga story), *Pagliacci* and Puccini's *Il tabarro* remain as prime examples of the genre. The *verismo* philosophy was to have a lasting influence on Puccini, though he was to extend and adapt it far beyond its original conception, especially in *La bohème* and most directly in *Tosca*, by fusing together spoken drama and musical development.

21

As his final examination piece for the Milan Conservatoire in July 1883, Puccini composed the *Capriccio sinfonico*. 'I felt inspired and composed it at home, in the street, in class, at the *Osteria Aida* or at the *Excelsior* of good old Signor Gigi where one ate without the silly pretence of being able to pay for it; I wrote on odd sheets, bits of paper and the margin of newspapers', he recounted later to his biographer Arnaldo Fraccaroli. This orchestral composition was performed by students conducted by Franco Faccio, who had directed the European première of *Aida*. The important critic Filippo Filippi reviewed it in the Milanese newspaper *La perseveranza*, commending its 'unity of style, personality and character', which, he felt, few other living composers could match. He identified in the composer a 'decisive and very rare musical temperament, one that is specifically symphonic'. In years to come, however, Puccini tried to suppress the work, largely, one suspects, because he borrowed extensively from it for *Edgar* and *La bohème*.

Puccini's other teacher at the Conservatoire had been Amilcare Ponchielli (1834-86), who was appointed professor of counterpoint in 1881, although he had won the competition for the post 14 years earlier, only to be denied it when Giulio Ricordi, Verdi's publisher, intervened to procure the post for Franco Faccio. Although Ponchielli had some success with his opera *I promessi sposi* based on Alessandro Manzoni's novel, he is chiefly remembered today as the composer of *La Giaconda*. Ironically, at one time Ricordi had high hopes that he might become Verdi's successor at the centre stage of Italy's operatic tradition. In the January of 1883, Ponchielli wrote to Puccini's mother, who had obviously requested his help in obtaining a Conservatoire post for her son at the end of his course, assuring her that he would 'omit nothing to assist him as soon as the opportunity presents itself to me'. That very year he encouraged Puccini to enter a competition for one-act operas sponsored by the wealthy Milanese music publisher, Edoardo Sonzogno, whose weekly magazine *La musica popolare* had printed Puccini's first published work in 1883, a song *Storiella d'amore*.

Trying to find his former pupil a librettist, Ponchielli approached Ferdinando Fontana, a writer and journalist, when the three met on a visit to Antonio Ghislanzoni, the librettist of *Aida*. The 33-year-old Fontana felt an immediate 'strong current of sympathy' for the aspiring composer and agreed to provide a libretto for a reduced sum, with a further payment should the opera win the prize.

Writing to his mother, Puccini described the libretto of

Pietro Mascagni conducting his famous *Cavalleria rusticana*.

Le Willis as 'a good subject... I really like it very much, there being ample scope in it for the descriptive, symphonic kind of music, which attracts me particularly because I think I ought to succeed in it.' The story has its origins in German myth; the *willis* of the title are elemental spirits of maidens, who haunt their faithless lovers and dance them to death. In this version Roberto is unfaithful to his betrothed, Anna, and, returning to her home in the Black Forest and finding her dead, is danced to death by her and her wraith companions. The tale is most well-known from Adolphe Adam's ballet *Giselle*, first produced in Paris in 1841. Catalani had also used the story for a successful opera *Elda* (1880), which he revised ten years later as *Loreley*. Fontana based his libretto on a short story by the French writer Alphonse Karr. Puccini worked on it throughout the autumn at Lucca, while earning some money by teaching. His pupils included Elvira Gemignani, the wife of a former school friend, now a wholesale grocer, who had suggested the idea of piano and singing lessons to his wife. They may well have known each other before her marriage. She was two years younger than Puccini, and by this time had two children, a daughter Fosca and a son, Renato. Undoubtedly striking, her tall, full figure, with her long hair in plaits on the top of her head, seems to have created an impression of statuesque dignity rather than overwhelming beauty. She did not have Giacomo's exuberance and love of life – a difference in their characters that did not bode well for the future – but it was different at the beginning; pupil and teacher were soon passionately in love.

Amilcare Ponchielli – known today almost exclusively for his opera *La Giaconda*.

Finishing the opera only just in time, Puccini submitted it for the competition without making a fair copy. Perhaps the judges made no attempt to decipher his scrawl, for he did not even receive an honourable mention, although Ponchielli was one of the panel. Determined that their work should receive a hearing, Fontana arranged for Puccini to play and sing excerpts at the *salon* of Marco Sala, a wealthy patron of the arts and an amateur musician. Among the guests were Giulio Ricordi, and Arrigo Boito, whose *Mefistofele* Puccini had studied as a student. It is, however, as the librettist for Verdi's final two operas that Boito is now chiefly remembered, and, in fact, he was working on *Otello* when he met the young composer at the *salon*. The assembled company was sufficiently impressed by the new opera to agree to raise the finance for a performance. Boito persuaded the manager of the Teatro dal Verme in Milan to stage it, while Ricordi offered to print the libretto free of charge. After the première on 31 May 1884, the composer sent his mother, who was ill, a telegram:

Arrigo Boito, renowned as the author of the libretti of Verdi's two last operas.

'Tumultuous success. All hopes surpassed. Eighteen calls. First finale encored three times. Am happy. Giacomo.' The reviews were excellent. Filippo Filippi castigated 'that wretched competition jury which accorded Puccini not even an honourable mention', and another critic hailed him as 'one of the most brilliant and most promising hopes of art'. 'We appear to have before us not a young student, but a Bizet or a Massenet,' declared *Il corriere della sera*, adding significantly: 'We sincerely believe that in Puccini we may have found the composer for whom Italy has long been waiting.'

On Ricordi's advice, Puccini recast the opera into two acts, giving it the Italian title *Le villi*. In this form, it was given with weaker forces and less acclaim at Turin. In a letter to Ricordi, Fontana described the singers as 'a lot of old crocks' and the orchestra as 'weak and lifeless'. However, even with 13 performances at La Scala, Milan under Franco Faccio with the soprano Romilda Pantaleoni – both of whom were to take part in the première of Verdi's *Otello* two years later – it was not a great success. The plot was essentially flawed: Fontana's libretto relegated the two decisive actions of the story, Roberto's infidelity and Anna's death, to narration between the acts, while the three central characters have little substance. Musically it is varied in quality: although there are signs of immaturity in, for example, the banal opening chorus, Puccini's deft touch is evident in Anna's frail tenderness and in the mixture of emotions revealed by the tenor in the duet and his long monologue. A disastrous production at Naples was followed by some performances in other countries, including one in Germany in 1892 conducted by Gustav Mahler, but *Le villi* is now rarely staged.

Of the ten set pieces that form the opera, the intermezzo was a particular success. The first half of this intermezzo, entitled 'The Desertion', deals with Anna's despair. The curtain was to be raised during it to show a funeral procession. Here, for the first time, Puccini demonstrates his ability to use stage effect to convey the emotional feelings of the characters, and tentatively explores what was to become a familiar theme of tragic guilt. The ballet, which forms the intermezzo's second half, tries perhaps to emulate the success of *Giselle*, and is very reminiscent of the overture to *Carmen*, which Puccini had described in a letter to his mother as 'a very beautiful opera'. Puccini's friend, Mascagni, was to win a later Sonzogno prize with *Cavalleria rusticana*, which, Puccini was always to feel, owed more than was acknowledged to his first opera.

The prima donna Teresa Stolz saw the La Scala production of *Le villi* and wrote a damning letter about it to Verdi. He,

Puccini, taken around the time of the première of *Le villi*.

however, had written to his friend Count Opprandino Arrivabene just after the première in slightly more complimentary terms, recognising that what he said might well be old fashioned and that 'every age has its own imprint':

I have heard the composer Puccini well spoken of. I have seen a letter in which he is highly praised. He follows the modern tendencies, which is natural, but he adheres to melody, which is neither modern nor antique. The symphonic element, however, appears to be predominant in him. Nothing wrong with that, but one needs to tread cautiously here. Opera is opera, and symphony is symphony and I do not believe it's a good thing to insert a piece of a symphony into an opera, simply for the pleasure of making the orchestra perform.

Though *Le villi* offers only glimpses of his future mastery of the operatic medium, Puccini had started out on his chosen career.

25

Chapter 2

Growing Pains

If the artist in Puccini were made of less stern stuff, he would look for another occupation. (Giulio Ricordi, after the failure of Puccini's second opera *Edgar*.)

Like Verdi before him, personal tragedy followed Puccini's first operatic triumph. He was able to take the laurel wreath he had received in Milan after the final performance of *Le villi* to show his mother on her deathbed, and was with her when she died in July 1884. He wrote to his elder sister: 'I think of her continually, and last night I also dreamed of her. So today I am even sadder than usual. Whatever triumph art may bring me, I shall never be very happy without my darling mother. Be comforted as much as you can and take courage – the courage which, so far, I have not been able to find myself.'

The death of his adored mother appears to have had a significant effect on his personal life. It is uncertain when his love affair with his former piano pupil Elvira Gemignani began, but by the middle of 1886 Elvira, unable to disguise any longer the fact that she was pregnant by her lover, left her husband and went to live in Milan with Giacomo. She took her daughter Fosca with her, but left the younger Renato with his aggrieved father. Since this was Catholic Italy of the late-nineteenth century, their elopement caused a great scandal in provincial Lucca.

Puccini, at 26, was dashingly handsome with a rakish style cultivated in his youth, accentuated by a moustache and thick chestnut hair. His left eyelid drooped, possibly because of his smoking, but his sensitive face and slim figure were undoubtedly irresistible to women. Renato Simoni, who later collaborated with him on the libretto of *Turandot*, was to describe him as 'straight, tall, with shoulders squared and hat at a slight angle, his hands in his pockets, his step slightly swinging but strongly rhythmical, with his strong, sunburned face, his

Puccini in Milan.

27

suggestion of rough shyness, and his good nature – sometimes boyish and sometimes touched with compassion.' Undoubtedly, Giacomo and Elvira were happy in those early days, before her possessiveness, her desire to dominate, and her jealousy, coupled with his infidelity and exclusion of her from the creative side of his life, soured their lifelong relationship. That he needed to run to Elvira's arms after his mother's death, yet later had to escape her strong-willed nature by numerous affaires with women of generally lower social and intellectual status are just two pieces of evidence of the profound, subconscious and continuing effect of his idealised relationship with his mother. After his father died when he was five, he had been brought up as his mother's favourite child in a largely feminine household – he had five sisters and a younger brother.

Four days after the première of *Le villi*, Puccini and Fontana had signed a contract for a second opera with Giulio Ricordi, the head of the music publishing house built up by his grandfather, Giovanni, and his father, Tito, into one of the most influential in the world. Its prestige had been enormously enhanced by the exclusive rights to the operas of Verdi, whom Giovanni and Tito Ricordi had supported and championed. Giulio's formal dress of frock coat, high collar and black tie underneath a well-trimmed beard certainly fitted his business position, yet it concealed artistic yearnings. He was an amateur composer, whose only opera was produced at Turin in 1910. Both Verdi and Puccini spoke appreciatively of his music. He also wrote poetry, articles and criticism for his house magazine the *Gazzetta musicale di Milano*, yet his most significant contribution to music was the promotion of 'his' composers. To be selected was not easy. He was a stern critic, though not infallible – he turned down works by Mascagni, Leoncavallo and Bizet. He had recently taken over the firm of his only serious rival in the music publishing business, Francesco Lucca, who had himself learnt the trade under Giulio Ricordi's grandfather. Lucca's wife, Giovannina, is still remembered for her astonishing proposal to Wagner that, before she would publish *Der Ring des Nibelungen* (the 'Ring Cycle') in Italy, he should consider shortening it 'so that it will last one single evening'. Giulio Ricordi, finding that Catalani was one of the composers he had inherited with Lucca's publishing interests, soon dropped him in favour of Puccini, providing his new protégé with a modest monthly income to supplement the royalties from *Le villi* while he worked on his second opera *Edgar*.

For this, Fontana originally produced a libretto in four acts based on a verse play by Alfred de Musset *La Coupe et les Lèvres*

Guilio Ricordi, Puccini's confidante and publisher.

29

Alfred de Musset, French poet, dramatist and novelist.

('There's many a Slip 'twixt Cup and Lip'), in which the gypsy orphan Tigrana lures the weak Edgar from the innocent Fidelia, eventually murdering her to prevent Edgar from returning to her. In his youthful enthusiasm Puccini described it to Ricordi as 'a work of such importance and such difficulty'. It bore a strong resemblance to the plot of Bizet's *Carmen* (1875), an opera which reflected the realism of French writers like Flaubert and Zola, and which Puccini had sneaked into La Scala free in order to see when he was a student. Fontana developed the melodramatic elements of the story – Edgar setting fire to his house, a mock funeral and the on-stage stabbing of the heroine. This had the merit of making Puccini extend his dramatic range, but the story was dated and the concept more suited to a grand opera such as Meyerbeer might have written.

Puccini did indeed find *Edgar* difficult to compose, labouring at it painfully and slowly from the summer of 1884 to the autumn of 1888. The use of material from several of his earlier works, including the *Messa di gloria*, the *Preludio in A*, the *Capriccio sinfonico* and an *Adagio* for string quartet reveals that original inspiration was hard for him to find. Already he was experiencing those times of despondency and despair that were to become so characteristic of his creative life. At this stage in his career he did not yet have the confidence to challenge librettists or demand a better subject. Ricordi began to put him under pressure to deliver the manuscript, while Elvira nagged him repeatedly, pointing out that Verdi had written *Rigoletto*, *Il trovatore* and *La traviata* in as many years. Giacomo was weighed down too by worries about how to support a mistress and two children – Elvira's daughter and their own baby, Antonio, born on 23 December 1886 after they had moved temporarily to Monza. Ricordi came to the rescue, agreeing to extend the monthly income, which Puccini jokingly referred to as '*la mia pensione*' (my pension). When, at last, the time for the first performance – on Easter Sunday, 21 April 1889 – drew near, he became very anxious. Writing to one of his sisters, Tomaide, nicknamed Dide, at 2am one Saturday night in 1889 – his usual custom was to work late into the night – he told her: 'All my household are well. I am living reasonably satisfactorily and am sufficiently tranquil and happy. I have many enemies here, but I hope to make them burst with envy and rage if God grants me long enough life.' His concern about the hostility that the success of *Le villi* had earned him reappears constantly in his letters of this time. However, as a student in Milan, he had made friends with the great tenor Francesco Tamagno, who had scored a major triumph by

30

creating the rôle of Otello in Verdi's opera at its première at La Scala in February 1887. Believing he was the person to bring *Edgar* to life, Puccini wrote him several letters trying to persuade him to sing the title rôle. 'It is in your power, if you are willing, to see to it that my work should be worthily appreciated', he wrote on 31 December 1888, and again, only two months before the first night, he wrote a pleading letter to Tamagno on 21 February 1889: 'There comes in the life of every man a decisive moment, and that is for me the success of *Edgar*. I cling to him who can save me, as one who has suffered shipwreck clings to the last plank. And that plank is you!'

His pleas were in vain, for Tamagno had just arranged to tour America. The cast was, nevertheless, a good one, including two of those who had taken part in the La Scala performances of *Le villi* – Romilda Pantaleoni as Tigrana and the conductor Franco Faccio. Yet it was not a success and was given only three performances. Pantaleoni told Boito that Tigrana was 'a cruel part which I do not feel', and, while recognising his technical advances since *Le villi*, the critics deemed it a failure. The best review came from Gramola in *Il corriere della sera*, who liked the orchestration and felt the best parts to be Fidelia's two arias in the last act, together with the funeral music, which Toscanini was to consider worthy to be used as a requiem at Puccini's funeral in 1924. The composer's attitude to the opera as a whole, however, changed in later life. Sending a vocal score to his English friend Sybil Seligman years later he re-wrote the title as: '***E D****io ti* ***G****u****AR****di da quest'opera*!' (And may God preserve you from this opera!). An annotation alongside the Act Two finale reads: 'the most horrible thing that has ever been written'; and where the crowd cry out 'Oh horror!' at the end of the opera, he comments: 'How right they are!' Only Fidelia's last two arias are exonerated from his ruthless self-criticism: he puts 'This is good!' in the margin.

Immediately after the first performance, Ricordi, having held what he described as an 'interminable discussion of almost five hours' with librettist and composer, wrote the next day to the latter:

Remember, Puccini, that you are at one of the critical and difficult moments of your artistic life... Your good Fontana has shown himself to be an eloquent orator, but a cavilling one. More of a philosopher-lawyer than a poet: the subtleties of his reasoning are admirable but they do not convince, they do not persuade. He holds to the same ideas as before... Yet, after all, it is the imagination and the personality of the musician which are everything. It is the musician who

The tenor Francesco Tamagno, who Puccini hoped would create the title rôle of his opera *Edgar*.

colours the work, who presents it to the public. Without him it is zero. Please understand, dear Puccini, that I am not in agreement with those who systematically belittle the libretto of *Edgar*. There are two effective acts [out of the four]: that is something. But it also contains much obscurity, many fallacies which derive from the theories of Fontana, who assumes that everybody thinks with *his* head. What impressed me all the more during the long discourse yesterday is that he will never benefit, not now, not later, from the experience of these days. Let us admit all the exaggerations, all the malice that the cruel critics have expended on the libretto: nonetheless there is some truth in what they say, and we must reckon with it.

The clear implication was that Fontana be ditched, and, although he offered to adapt Oscar Wilde's *A Florentine Tragedy* 18 years later, Puccini never used him again. By contrast, facing a vote at a shareholders' meeting that Puccini himself be dropped, Ricordi continued to support him, increasing the 'pension' with the promise that he would make good the debt himself if the composer did not prove to be a sound investment. 'If they wish to close the door on Giacomo Puccini, I myself will exit with him by the same door.'

Edgar was revised for some projected performances at La Scala in the spring of 1890, though these never took place because of the illness of the leading tenor. However, the following year it was given 13 highly-appreciated performances at the delightful little Teatro Giglio in Lucca, about which Puccini wrote enthusiastically to his sister Nitteti, whose husband had recently died. Subsequently, Puccini further revised it into a three-act version, first performed at Ferrara on 28 February 1892, and then in March at the Teatro Reál in Madrid. When the tenor for this production dropped out, Puccini again wrote to Tamagno, who was to be in Madrid anyway:

I take my courage in both hands and make bold to address to you a request – to ask you a very great favour which, if granted, will be of immense advantage to my career... *Edgar* should have been given at the Teatro Reál last year, but time and circumstances to do with the repertoire prevented this. At the time I had been given the formal promise by the management...that this work of mine would be produced during the current season; rehearsals were already at an advanced stage – we were in fact near the date of the première – when I was notified that Durot [who had sung Edgar at Lucca] had dissolved his contract and so my poor *Edgar* was left without a protagonist and without hope of a performance! Tetrazzini [Eva, not her more famous sister Luisa] and Pasqua [Gisueppina Pasqua, Verdi's first Mistress Quickly] were to have been the other principal interpreters. This was for me a most ruinous disaster, as I had counted on the production of *Edgar* to give me an uplift which I needed most direly, morally as well as materially. Hence my request, which I make bold to address to you, to sing the very important part of the protagonist. Courage and audacity are needed, what! But since I know you to be so kind-hearted, I took the liberty of putting this idea to you. Shall I be granted this request? I confess that I hope so. The opera has now been reduced to three acts. Two years ago you saw the music and studied it so that it will not be new to you and give you little trouble to learn it. If you accept, you can be sure of my immutable and unlimited gratitude. Among the many misfortunes that have befallen me, this would at least be my good luck! I'm writing to you just as my heart dictates it, jotting down the words as they leap into my head. I am so excited when I think that perhaps – who knows? – you will sing my stuff!

In fact, a great deal more cajoling was required from both Puccini and Ricordi before Tamagno did agree. Eva Tetrazzini and Giuseppina Pasqua took the female rôles as planned. Puccini was given several curtain calls and introduced to the Queen of Spain and other members of the royal family who were present. Nevertheless, it was a not a great success. After yet more revision, Puccini did see the opera again in Buenos Aires in 1905, but dismissed it as 'warmed-up soup. I have always said so. What is wanted is a subject which palpitates with life and is believable – not trash.'

What Puccini had grasped was that opera-goers were not insulated from the enormous changes that had gathered momentum in the closing decades of the nineteenth century. This was a period of significant development in understanding by human beings of their environment and their ability to control and use it to their advantage. There were notable advances in all fields of scientific thought, which had repercussions not only on the way people lived and worked, but on how the intellectually minded regarded themselves.

Caricature of Charles Darwin in *The London Sketch Book* of 1874.

The remarkable ferment of ideas in the last 30 years of the century owed much to the work of two men. Charles Darwin's *The Origin of Species by Means of Natural Selection* (1859), by demolishing the biblical concepts of separately created and distinct species of plants and animals, had provoked an enormous furore, of which the celebrated dispute between T.H.Huxley and Bishop Wilberforce at the British Association meeting at Oxford in 1860 was just one example. In *The Descent of Man* (1871), Darwin made explicit his thesis that humans, like all other forms of life, had evolved by natural selection from earlier, more primitive forms. While Darwin examined the origins of human beings in pre-history, Karl Marx, in *Das Kapital* (1867), focused attention on their present and future by trying to look systematically at the economic principles of industrial civilisation and the dynamics of social history, which, he argued, made proletarian revolution inevitable. At Marx's funeral, his disciple Friedrich Engels declared: 'Just as Darwin discovered the law of development of organic nature, so Marx discovered the law of development of human history.' Both thinkers had revolutionised thought, challenging accepted ideas about the nature of human life. Puccini was right that opera, like the other arts, was likely to touch the spirit of the age when it was not only about individual human experience and emotion, but was also rooted in the reality of the world in which those individuals lived.

Verdi had written for an audience craving a national identity,

Karl Marx in London, 1849.

to whom historical dramas with their themes of justice, truth, patriotism and heroism spoke directly. Puccini was writing for an emerging *bourgeoisie* at a time of relative prosperity. Although much of Italy remained structured around a backward, agricultural economy, the process of industrialisation and urbanisation was changing the face of her towns and cities. This pace of change was there for all to see in the Milan Industrial Fair of 1881. It was held in the new Galleria Vittorio Emanuele constructed of iron and glass, the dome being lit by two thousand gas jets which were ignited by a mechanical engine travelling round the inside of the dome carrying a flame.

In fact, the revolution in lighting had a very direct effect on opera audiences. The 1880s saw the building of the first large-scale electricity-generating stations following the pioneering work of Michael Faraday (1791-1867) in establishing the principles of electro-magnetism. When theatres had been lit by candles, since the lights could neither be dimmed nor put out, audiences had consisted largely of the upper classes who came to be seen and who consequently chattered throughout the performance. The introduction of gas lighting meant that lights could at least be dimmed. Then, with the spread of Thomas Edison's electric lighting in the 1880s, auditorium lights could be turned off at the flick of a switch with the result that audiences changed dramatically. The upper classes, who had come as part of the social round, ceased to come in significant numbers. They were gradually replaced by genuine music lovers, mainly of the middle-classes, who were keen supporters of opera performances in the cities and towns where they lived. In their turn, through their responses they exerted an influence on the composers and librettists whose works they came to hear. Such connections between science and the arts were epitomised in Puccini's own life, by his later meetings with Marconi, and Edison, who sent him a signed photograph in 1920 inscribed: 'Men die and governments change, but the songs of *La bohème* will live for ever.'

It was the French novelist, Émile Zola, who seemed to have captured the way in which the spirit of the age was influencing literature, including libretti, which were often based on plays or novels. At a Congress in Aix-en-Provence in 1866, he declared:

Gone is the time when the reader was kept in suspense by a complicated dramatic but improbable story; the sole object is to register human facts, to lay bare the mechanism of body and soul. The plot is simplified; the first person one comes across will do as a hero; examine it and you are sure to find a straight-forward drama which allows full play to all the machinery of emotion and passion.

Above left:
Electric stage lighting replacing gas at the Paris Opéra given in *L'illustration,* 1887.

Above right:
Electric light at the Paris Opéra, 1882.

The Galleria Vittorio Emanuele, Milan– the venue for the Industrial Fair of 1881.

After the first performances of *Edgar*, the dejected Puccini wondered whether to follow his brother, Michele, to Argentina, where he had emigrated after trying unsuccessfully to set up as a music teacher. 'If you can find work for me after *Edgar*, I shall come. But not to Buenos Aires, to the interior amongst the redskins!' he wrote on 6 February 1890. There were a large number of Italians in South America, which is why Puccini operas were often performed there soon after their first appearance in Italy. In the same letter Giacomo told his brother that he had enjoyed a production of Wagner's *Die Meistersinger von Nürnberg* (given as *I maestri cantori di Norimberga*) at La Scala, though it had 'bored the Milanese audiences'. In 1889 he had gone with Franco Faccio to Bayreuth to consult about cuts to the opera for the Italian performances. On a lighter note, he told Michele that 'Buffalo Bill has been here. I enjoyed the show. They are a company of North Americans with some Red Indians and buffaloes. They perform magnificent feats of shooting and give realistic presentations of scenes that have happened on the frontier.'

Creditors, including some his brother had left behind, added

Puccini's brother, Michele.

to Puccini's worries, as he explained in another letter to Michele, probably written in April 1890:

The chemist is worrying me and I shall have to pay your account of twenty-five lire. I am absolutely down on the rocks. I don't know how to go on... If I could find means of making money, I would come where you are. Is there any chance for me there? I would leave everything behind and go... The theatres here are stingy and, because of the critics, the public becomes more and more difficult. God help me! I am ready, absol:utely ready to come, if you write. I shall come and we'll manage *somehow*.

Michele's reply was strongly discouraging:

Dear Giacomo,
I warn you – do not come here! You cannot imagine what I have been through. What a life! I left Buenos Aires, where I worked like a slave, with nothing to show for it on account of the high cost of living. Then they told me that in the province of Yoyoy [Jujuy] I would obtain a position teaching voice, piano and Italian for 300 *scudi* a month. I crossed the Andes, and after innumerable sufferings came at last to Yoyoy. Of course, as you might expect, the place is full of Lucchese [people from Lucca]... But America does not suit me. If the gold market improves, I shall return to Lucca. Meanwhile I am a little worried by the epidemic of influenza. My classroom is empty.

It was not, however, influenza which Michele need have feared. When Giacomo was able to pay for his brother to return home in 1893, it was too late. In Jujuy, Michele had a love affair with the wife of a local politician, had injured the senator in a subsequent duel and fled to Rio de Janeiro, where there was an epidemic of yellow fever. He contracted the disease and died far from his homeland after much suffering, just like the fictional heroine Manon, whose story would soon bring his brother his first great success.

Chapter 3

On the Threshold of Success

Forward, forward, and quickly! (Giulio Ricordi in a letter to Puccini about *Manon Lescaut*, 2 August 1892.)

Even before the revision of *Edgar* into three acts, Ricordi had begun to make suggestions for a third opera, encouraging others to provide potential libretti. From the playwright Giuseppe Giacosa he commissioned a scenario set in Russia, but Puccini responded in a manner that revealed his growing self-confidence and understanding of what was right for him and for his audience:

The French writer, Abbé Prévost.

I fear the subject is not suitable for me; I am afraid that I shall not succeed in writing the kind of music it should have. I wonder if you could find a way of suggesting to Giacosa, without hurting him, that he should leave it alone for the present?... We should look for, and certainly find, something more poetic, more pleasing, and less gloomy, and with a little more nobility of conception. That Russia of his frightens me and, to tell the truth, does not convince me!

Shakespeare had already provided the inspiration for several Italian operas, most notably *Otello* by both Rossini (1816) and Verdi (1887), *Macbeth* also by Verdi (1847) and Franco Faccio's *Amleto* (1865); so another playwright, Marco Praga, perhaps bearing in mind the rumours that Verdi was considering a *Falstaff*, tried to interest Puccini in the King Henry plays as a possible source.

Puccini was not, however, to be tempted. He had read and been attracted by *L'Histoire du Chevalier des Grieux et de Manon Lescaut* by the Abbé Prévost (1697-1763), a rather disreputable French Benedictine priest, who had found it necessary to flee from the troubles into which his love of the pleasures of the world had led him. It was probably while in London that he wrote his seven-volume novel *Mémoires et aventures d'un homme de qualité*, the last volume of which contains the story that caught the composer's attention. Puccini was by no means the first to have noted the potential of the story. It had been made into a French play in 1765, and was used as the basis for a ballet by Halévy in 1830 and an opera by Auber in 1856, the last two written by that most prolific Frenchman Eugène Scribe – whose works take up 76 volumes and whose opera libretti credits include not only 38 by Auber, but also Rossini's *Le Comte Ory*, Bellini's *La sonnambula*, Donizetti's *L'elisir d'amore*, Cilea's *Adriana Lecouvreur*, Halévy's *La Juive*, Meyerbeer's *Les Huguenots* and *L'Africaine*, and Verdi's *Les vêpres siciliennes* and *Un ballo in maschera*. The most famous version of the Prévost story was by Jules Massenet (1842-1912), professor of advanced composition at the Paris Conservatoire, whose *Manon*, first produced at the Paris Opéra-Comique in 1884, was his greatest triumph. Of all Massenet's 27 operas, *Manon* most quickly entered and remained in the repertoire of the world's opera houses.

Though Massenet's *Manon* was not performed in Italy until 1893, Puccini clearly knew of it, in spite of the fact that one of his early biographers attempted to deny it. 'Manon is a heroine I believe in, and therefore she cannot fail to win the hearts of the public,' he wrote to Ricordi in 1889. He peremptorily dismissed the idea that writing on the same subject would be a disadvantage: 'Massenet feels it as a Frenchman, with the powder and the minuets. I shall feel it as an Italian, with desperate passion [*con passione disperata*].' His new-found confidence even extended to the text, so that he wrote to Ricordi: 'No idiotic librettist must be allowed to ruin the story. I shall certainly put my hand to the making of the libretto.'

However, his pretensions as a dramatist soon faded and the search for a librettist began. Ricordi had been impressed with the libretti of two as yet unperformed operas submitted to him by Puccini's contemporary Ruggero Leoncavallo, who wrote his own libretti, but Puccini wanted to work with an acquaintance of his own, Marco Praga, a playwright of some distinction. Meeting him in the Galleria Vittoria Emanuele one evening, Puccini persuaded him to attempt the task, in spite of the fact that he had never previously written a libretto. Praga agreed because of 'the friendship and admiration I felt for Puccini', on condition that he could enrol Domenica Oliva, author of a recently-published collection of poems, to write the verses, and agreement was reached in the summer of 1889. The composer asked Praga to base his work on the novel rather than the French libretto, so that the work would not be influenced by Scribe's treatment, and to bear in mind that he intended it to be 'an *opéra comique* in the classical sense of the term', namely a

lyrical romantic opera with spoken dialogue. Praga later
recounted how, since Puccini had seemed delighted with his
suggested division into four acts, he had gone ahead with
writing the plot and had shown it to Puccini and Giulio
Ricordi, who approved it. Domenico Oliva then wrote the
verses and the libretto was completed by early 1890. Although
Puccini finished Act One by March, he then began to find fault
with the libretto, in particular demanding an embarkation
scene at Le Havre for the end of the third act. Praga recalled:

In the summer, I went with Puccini and Oliva to Cernobbio, where
the Ricordi family was spending the summer, and we read the poem.
Paolo Tosti [a well-known song writer] was present at the reading.
The success of it was complete. Tosti said that he had never read a
more beautiful or more effective libretto. It was the *opéra comique* of
which Puccini had dreamed.

Back in Milan, we concluded our agreement and Puccini departed
with his, or rather with our, manuscript. Things could not have been

41

better. But such a pleasant state of affairs was of short duration. A few months after, the composer was no longer satisfied with the plot or with the division of the acts. He could no longer feel that it was an *opéra comique*.

On further consideration, Puccini wanted to eliminate the second act, partly because he did not want to be accused of copying Massenet. Praga did not approve and backed out, with some justification, since the omission of the act depicting the lovers' happiness becoming soured by poverty removes the explanation for the transformation of the innocent Manon of Act One into the courtesan of Act Two living in the house of the wealthy Geronte. (Evidence of Puccini's original plan to write a comic opera survives in the scenes in the second act with the hairdresser, a group of singers and the dancing master, to which the Marschallin's *levée* in *Der Rosenkavalier* by Richard Strauss (1911) bears a strong resemblance). Leoncavallo was then called in to re-write Act Two, but after producing an outline he too gave up in order to devote himself to his own composition and writing. In the meantime, Oliva and Puccini had been working together on the idea of a third act depicting the embarkation of the prostitutes at Le Havre, with Des Grieux arriving and deciding to sail with Manon into exile, but this working relationship, too, did not survive long. Faced with a catalogue of detailed criticisms of his text sent by Puccini to Ricordi, Oliva lost patience and resigned as well. Ricordi then approached another young playwright, Luigi Illica (1857-1919). He re-fashioned the embarkation scene, which eventually became an act in its own right preceded by an intermezzo, on a decision taken in the summer of 1892 to drop the original Act Two altogether and replace it with the first scene of the third act much enlarged. Eventually, Illica persuaded Giacosa to assist him and thus was born a collaboration that was to provide the libretti for Puccini's three most popular operas, *La bohème*, *Tosca* and *Madama Butterfly*.

Giuseppe Giacosa (1847-1906) was a leading Italian playwright, as well as being a poet, essayist, writer of short stories, professor of literature and drama at the Milan Conservatoire, and editor of the foremost Italian literary periodical *La lettura*. Of his 32 plays, two at least had won him international recognition – *Tristi amori* (Sad Loves) (1887) and *La comtesse de Chaillant* (The Countess of Chaillant) (1891), in which the leading rôles were taken respectively by Eleonora Duse and Sarah Bernhardt, two of the leading actresses of their day. Because he was short and bulky, with a large paunch, Puccini was later to nickname him 'the Giacosan Buddha'. He brought

42

Puccini with Giacosa and Illica, two of the five librettists involved in his opera *Manon Lescaut.*

to the partnership a constant search for literary excellence, so that, when translating Illica's prose text into verse, he worked in painstaking detail and with a consequential slowness that could be infuriating to his collaborators.

By contrast, Illica was fast and prolific. His own plays may have been of less merit, but he made his mark as the author of many libretti, including Catalani's *La Wally* (1892), Giordano's *Andrea Chénier* (1896) and Mascagni's *Iris* (1898). Like Puccini, he had a great sense of the theatrical moment and his imaginative invention was a counterbalance to Giacosa's literary vision. His extravagant life-style, which often landed him in financial difficulties, was but one manifestation of his unpredictable and impulsive character – when a boy, he had run away to sea. His arrogance could be expressed in biting criticism or furious rages, leading on one occasion to a sabre duel with the editor of the *Gazzetta dell'Emilia*, in which he lost part of his left ear. He was at his best when working with Giacosa, where his momentary enthusiasms were

43

balanced by the weight of authority his more serious partner brought to their deliberations. In an obituary of his colleague in October 1906 for *La lettura*, Illica was to describe their discussions thus:

Those sessions of ours!... Real battles in which there and then entire acts were torn to pieces, scene after scene sacrificed, ideas abjured which only a moment ago had seemed bright and beautiful; thus was destroyed in a minute the work of long and painful months. Giacosa, Puccini, Giulio Ricordi and I – we were a quartet because Giulio Ricordi, who was presumed to preside, would always leave his presidential chair and descend into our semi-circle which was extremely narrow (two metres in circumference and rendered more narrow still and more close and uncomfortable by the mighty person of Giacosa) to become one of the most obstinate and most vigorous belligerents... Giacosa was, for us, the equilibrium; in dark moments he was the sun, on stormy days the rainbow... In that uproar of voices expressing different views and conceptions, Giacosa's voice was the delightful, persuasive song of the nightingale... And Puccini? After each session, he had to run to the manicurist to have his finger-nails attended to: he had bitten them off, down to the bone!

Illica did not approve of the final act of *Manon Lescaut*, set in America; he later confided to Sir Thomas Beecham that he had felt it to be an anticlimax, but Puccini had written the music and was determined to use it.

Ricordi was immensely relieved to have found at last in this partnership those who could complete the libretto of *Manon*. 'The two poets are working with great enthusiasm,' he wrote to Puccini on 18 May 1891, 'and it is indeed a pleasure to do business with two people so cultivated and charming.' Even in these early days of the collaboration, the publisher was heavily involved in the negotiations between composer and librettists, making comments and even some modest contributions, constantly writing notes to Puccini about details, and urging him on to complete the opera. He even used the 79-year-old Verdi as a spur to his protégé:

I went to Verdi's for one day on business. That man is a marvel. I know it and yet I cannot get over it with the years. It will give you pleasure to know that both Verdi and his wife [the former prima donna, Giuseppina Strepponi, with whom he had lived for 11 years before their marriage – a not dissimilar situation to Puccini and Elvira] have interested themselves in you, asked me for news about *Manon*, if you will have good performers, etc., etc. They wish you success.

Eventually, after three years' gestation, the opera was

View of Turin (1889), where *Manon Lescaut* was premièred.

finished in October 1892, although it was some time before Ricordi and Puccini agreed to call it *Manon Lescaut* to distinguish it from Massenet's opera *Manon*, and, because of the multiplicity of authorship, to give no credit to the five librettists. It was first performed at the Teatro Regio in Turin on 1 February 1893 only a few days before Verdi's *Falstaff* was first performed at La Scala, a fact which had no doubt been in Ricordi's mind in suggesting an alternative venue for the Puccini first night, lest direct comparisons were drawn. Also, he probably feared the Milan audience might be prejudiced by their memories of *Edgar*. From Turin, where he was supervising rehearsals, Giacomo wrote to Elvira: 'Let them say what they want – this time I have a feeling that I have done a successful piece of work. Here, everybody is mad about it. Nevertheless, the execution will be wretched, because the voices can hardly be heard.'

Expectations were high; the performance was a sell-out and critics came from all over Italy to see the new opera. The première was a wild success, though time was to prove it to be the only first night when public and critics united in their acclaim of a new opera by Puccini. He even had to appear on stage in Act One to acknowledge the thunderous applause for the tenor aria, while, at the end, he joined the singers for about 30 curtain calls. 'In my lengthy career as a journalist, it has rarely happened to me to be present at so important an evening as last night's,' wrote the critic of *La perseveranza*, while

45

Giuseppe Depanis of the *Gazzetta Piemontese*, calling Puccini 'one of the strongest talents among young Italian composers of opera,' went on to record that 'critics and the public were of one mind in paying tribute to, and in acclaiming, a robust opera of a young Italian maestro, one who has done honour to his name and to his country. Art has no boundaries, to be sure. Nonetheless, national pride is legitimate: last night was a good night for art and for Italy.' The opportunist Ricordi linked the hire of the orchestral parts for the opera with *Falstaff*, so that it was advantageous for impresarios to give both operas together, the younger composer thus benefiting from the association with Verdi's comic masterpiece of his last years. Following a suggestion by Illica, this published score contained a new finale to Act One, replacing a conventional ensemble for soloists and chorus with some dialogue and a chorus of the students.

Although distinct echoes of Wagner, particularly *Tristan und Isolde*, can be heard in *Manon Lescaut*, Puccini had found his own voice. This was recognised by Giovanni Pozza, critic of the Milanese *Il corriere della sera*, who could not resist a dig at other composers of the '*giovane scuola*' like Leoncavallo and Mascagni: 'Puccini instinctively draws back from Wagner's mystic profundity yet, for all that, he is not given to making concessions to trivial melodrama.' With the reservation that the brass was used too stridently at times, Pozza commended the orchestra's significant rôle, which 'the modern style now demands and which is as it should be', and concluded:

Between *Edgar* and this *Manon*, Puccini has vaulted an abyss. *Edgar* can be said to have been a necessary preparation, all redundancies, all flashes and indications; *Manon* is the work of the genius, conscious of his own power, master of his art, a creator and perfector of it. *Manon* can be ranked among the classical operas. Puccini's genius is truly Italian.

There is no doubt that the three years it took to compose *Manon Lescaut* were well spent by Puccini. These days he may be remembered chiefly for his later operas, but the compositional advance he made to *Manon Lescaut* was to prove the most significant one of his career. Already his melodies have begun to flow fluently, the boundaries between recitative and aria have disappeared, and his sure eye for theatrical moment is clearly in evidence. The action, involving the personal lives of a few people, is set in the real world, where others leading diverse lives witness and comment on the events of the central characters – for instance, in the inn courtyard or on the Le Havre quayside, or even in the world of the *salon* with its

46

Real-life emigration scene at Le Havre, 1887.

profusion of hangers-on. Like Verdi before him, Puccini was adept at the big choral scene. The townsfolk on the quayside, who express a wide variety of individual reactions to the scene, provide the perfect backdrop for the desperate words of farewell uttered by Manon and Des Grieux against the harsh reality of the Sergeant's roll call. It does not matter that this opera is set in the eighteenth century. The growth of the young lovers' infatuation, depicted first in the orchestra, then in their hesitant exchanges until it pours out in unfettered melody demonstrates the composer's ability to convey the depths of human emotion. The way in which Des Grieux gives up his life for the love of a girl whose worth, in conventional terms, turns out to be questionable, touched the hearts of the first-night audience because Puccini's music re-created the overpowering feelings of love, hate, hope and despair that they knew from their own lives. As the critic Pozza said, Puccini was able to articulate Italian sensuality and even – he used a potent word – 'our paganism' – strong but suppressed feelings, desires, hopes and fears, which, perhaps, many felt could only be safely acknowledged in a theatrical performance.

47

The dominant mood of pessimism, disillusionment and despair, evident in *Manon Lescaut* and most of Puccini's subsequent operas, captured the predominant mood of the period, often referred to as *fin de siècle*. The effect of Marx and Darwin was not simply to cause people to examine the reality of their outer world, but also to question long-held moral, social and aesthetic values – what Nietzsche called 'the transvaluation of all values' – and to probe the inner world as well. In an age where scientific progress was bringing into fresh focus the harsh realities of physical and mental disease, poverty and other ugly sides of life, opera, like literature and drama, began to see as its proper subject not only the finer shades of feeling and sensibility, but the darker sides of cruelty, eroticism and sexual perversion. Nietzsche's epithet 'the refinement of cruelty belongs to the springs of art' could well have been uttered by Puccini's cynical protagonist in *Tosca*, Baron Scarpia. Friedrich Nietzsche, who wrote a book a year from *The Birth of Tragedy* in 1872 until he finally went insane in 1888, has been called by the historian John Trevelyan an 'intense, brooding, introspective genius [who] conceived a

Manon Lescaut at La Scala Milan, 1894.

philosophy of life and death that defied all existing and conventional doctrines'. 'The nature and the degree of a man's sexuality reaches up to the last recesses of his mind,' wrote Nietzsche 30 years before Freud. In *Manon Lescaut*, Puccini explores the way in which two people's lives are eventually brought to the depths of degradation and despair by their sexuality; but it is the power of his music that explores and reveals the 'last recesses' of their minds. Some have maintained that a weakness of the opera is that the first two acts contain all the gaiety, while the last two acts are filled with despair and gloom. Although this may be a failing of the opera when viewed as a dramatic construction, there is a profound significance in the move away from the pleasure-seeking atmosphere of a bygone era towards the mood of pessimism prevalent in the closing decade of the century.

The opera had been written in several places, as Puccini searched for a home in which to settle with his family. 'To tear me away from the country is to tear away part of my life,' he wrote in April 1890 when he was still living in 'this horrible soul-destroying Milan'. In the early summer, he rented a chalet

1890s street scene, Milan.

for himself, Elvira and the children in Vacallo, on the border with Switzerland. Leoncavallo was composing there too, and left the new arrivals in no doubt as to the subject of the opera he was working on, by fixing to his door a large picture of a clown (*pagliaccio*). So, a few days later, Giacomo hung out of his window a drawing of a hand (*manon* in Italian). After staying in Vacallo for the summer and winter, the family split up, since Puccini had to go back to Lucca, in order to be able to reach Milan more easily to consult his operatic collaborators. To avoid further malicious gossip, Elvira took the children to stay with her sister in Florence.

From Lucca, Puccini wrote her affectionate letters, calling her by a variety of pet names – 'Elviretta', 'Piglet', 'Birdie', 'Little Pea' and 'Little Mouse' (*'Topizia'*) – while he signed himself *'Topizio'*. Yet, in the spring of 1891, the first serious rift in their relationship occurred. There is no evidence that he had been unfaithful to her at that time, but a rumour evidently reached her, evoking a letter from Giacomo, in which he tried to convince her of the falsity of the story and stop her rushing to Lucca: 'You know how hard I must work, as everything depends on my work, and I don't have the peace of mind that I need; I beg of you, think of me and make the sacrifice of being patient and staying where you belong – don't worry about me – I am and will always be your *Topizio*, and the time will come when we shall be calm and happy...' His explanations proved insufficient to stem Elvira's suspicions, so he had to write to her again in June after he had obviously received a fairly fiery response to his earlier letter:

Why don't you remain as calm as possible? What reasons can there be for you to be so upset on my account? You say that you have to tell me *certain things* in person. For my part, I have nothing to blame myself for; I have always acted and always will act loyally toward you – no subterfuges, no idea of leaving you, of betraying you. My only desire is to be able to finish *Manon* in peace. I have committed myself (if I weren't to keep my word, I should be ruined) and it must be ready for Turin next Carnival. In November, if we can wait so long, I'll come and fetch you to resume our life – to live together eternally with our baby until it is time for him to enter boarding school... Have faith in me; good God, what more can I tell you? Every day the same complaints, the same oaths, and you know me well enough not to have any doubts. If you continue, I shall be hurt. You know I am your love and you are my only and true, holy love...

Sadly, while this may well have been true at the time, their relationship was to deteriorate further over the next decade.

Evidently deciding he must take some action to reassure

Elvira, Puccini found the family a home where they could live
together by September 1891. In 1884, he had discovered the
little fishing village of Torre del Lago (the Tower by the Lake)
on the shores of Lake Massaciuccoli, about 15 miles from
Lucca, on the plain between the foothills of the Apuan Alps
and the Mediterranean sea, and it was here he was able to rent
part of the house of the estate manager of the Marchese Carlo
Ginori-Lisci, the owner of the lake. The Puccinis soon moved
to a large villa nearby, which they rented from a Sienese
nobleman, Count Gratonelli, but, once the royalties from *La
bohème* put him on a better financial footing, he bought a large
property at Monsagrati near Chiatri in the hills above Torre.
Unlike Verdi, who devoted much time to the running of his
estate at Sant'Agata, Puccini had no interest in agricultural
management; it was the remoteness of the place that appealed
to him, as he expressed in a letter to Ricordi in July 1898:

51

I am in a hideous, hateful place, amidst woods and pine trees which shut off all view, closed in by mountains and lighted by a broiling sun, with not a breath of wind. But the evenings are delicious and the nights enchanting. I work from ten in the evening till four in the morning. The house is large and indoors one is very comfortable. All in all, I am very happy to have fled to this tedious place where the human being is the exception. We are really alone.

Their son Antonio, or Tonio as he was known, was at this time at boarding school in Milan, but Elvira and her daughter Fosca came to dislike Monsagrati intensely, eventually persuading Puccini to leave it, though he always blamed them for turning him against it. He kept it on as a solitary retreat, and later bought another villa for the same purpose at Abetone in the Apennines. The move from Monsagrati was possible because he had at last been able to build his own house at Torre del Lago, on the site of one he had bought from his former landlord, Venanzio, and then razed to the ground.

Torre del Lago, which he called his supreme joy and paradise, held three immense attractions for him – solitude for composition, a refuge from singers, publishers, librettists and admirers, and a paradise for wildfowling. True Tuscan that he was, he adored going out at dawn to shoot pheasant, duck and other waterbirds on the Lake and around its reed beds and

Lake Massaciuccoli Torre at del Lago.

bulrushes. The ground floor of the house at Torre is mainly taken up with his spacious study with its specially-dampened piano (because he composed so much at night) and his gunroom full of his large collection of guns, equipment, stuffed birds and photographs of hunting expeditions. This passion was to lead him into some tricky situations. Once, he and Giovanni Manfredi, his usual companion, were mistaken at night in their boat for poachers and nearly shot by the Marchese's gamekeepers. Another time, he and a friend were arrested on the further shore for trespassing, shooting during the closed season, and being without a firearms permit. When he heard of it, Ricordi, who had been concerned lest 'your passion for birds seduce you away from music,' wrote a jocular letter saying that he hoped Puccini would be locked up in prison with a piano, so he could 'blast forth gunshots of melody' and actually finish *La bohème*, which he was engaged on at the time. Although he was found not guilty of the charges against him, owing to the wiliness of his defending counsel, Puccini still did not apply for a hunting permit until the end of 1894. Despite this, the two men became firm friends, and *La bohème* is dedicated to the Marchese. The male pastime of hunting also gave him an excuse to escape from his home. Certainly his pattern of composing mainly in the evening and at night, with shooting expeditions in the early morning, meetings during the day and much time spent away, was not conducive to a settled family life.

At the time of *Manon Lescaut*, however, the house at Torre was still only a dream for the future, though Puccini's new-found national and international fame was making such ambitions seem more realistic. In 1893, the year of its première, *Manon* was performed widely, in many Italian opera houses and in Buenos Aires, Rio de Janeiro, St Petersburg, Madrid and Hamburg. The next year, it was given in Lisbon, Budapest, Prague, London, Montevideo, Philadelphia and Mexico. Yet Puccini remained essentially shy in public and tended to avoid having to speak on public occasions. When asked to make a speech at a banquet in his honour a week after the première, he couldn't do better than '*Grazie a tutti*' (Thank you everyone), even though he had written notes on his shirt cuff. After Catalani's premature death in August, Puccini's former teacher, Bazzini, offered him the professorship of composition at the Milan Conservatoire, while Venice tried to tempt him to become Director of the famous Liceo Benedetto Marcello. His was not the kind of mind to be tied to institutions, however prestigious; besides which, the royalties he was now receiving meant he could not only afford to turn such offers down, but even to repay the firm of Ricordi the debt of nine years' worth of monthly advances, proving Giulio's faith to have been well founded. He was also able to buy back his father's house in Lucca that had been sold after his mother's death.

He began to travel more widely now, since he was always keen to attend new productions of his works. He returned to Germany for *Manon Lescaut*, which he did not actually see as the opening performance was postponed, but the *Berliner Börse Courier* commented that 'he breathes the same fervent breath as Wagner, but maintains gifts of absolute originality'. In Rome, he was given 27 curtain calls in the presence of the Grand Duchess Catherine of Russia, while, in January 1894, he returned to Naples where, as a report in the paper *Roma* put it, 'the city which had been so hostile (perhaps unjustly) to the author of *Le villi*, wanted to make honourable amends to that severe judgment, demonstrating not only faith in his merits, but also wanting to reconfirm the triumph achieved by a powerful opera in almost every theatre in the peninsula.' A performance in Pisa, conducted by the young Arturo Toscanini, was followed by a trip to Budapest and Vienna, and then in May to London for performances at Covent Garden. The critic of *The Standard* was positive: 'Signor Puccini possesses the gift of melody, is a master of orchestration, and has rare comprehension of dramatic effects.' George Bernard Shaw, in a review in *The World*, gave a very perceptive analysis:

The first act, which is as gay and effective and romantic as the opening of any version of *Manon* need be, is also unmistakably symphonic in its treatment. There is genuine symphonic modification, development, and occasionally combination of the thematic material, all in a dramatic way, but also in a musically homogeneous way, so that the act is really a single movement with episodes, instead of being a succession of separate numbers... Puccini shows no signs of atrophy of the melodic faculty: he breaks out into catching melodies quite in the vein of Verdi.

Shaw put into words what many had begun to feel: 'Puccini looks to me more like the heir of Verdi than any of his rivals.'

Chapter 4

Genius will Out

La bohème, even as it leaves little impression on the minds of the audience, will leave no great trace upon the history of our lyric theatre. (Carlo Bersezio in *La stampa*, 1896.)

For his next opera, Puccini toyed first with two other subjects before settling on *La bohème*. In a letter to his brother, written while he was still working on *Manon Lescaut*, he told him he was thinking of writing an opera about the Buddha – a most unlikely subject, and indeed, nothing more was heard of it. Instead, he became very keen to set *La lupa* (The She-Wolf), one of Giovanni Verga's Sicilian short stories. Puccini was

Square of the Elephant, Catania, Sicily.

probably spurred on by the knowledge that another of these tales had been the source of the plot for Mascagni's one-act opera *Cavalleria rusticana*, which had achieved phenomenal success in 1890 after winning the Sonzogno prize, the same competition in which *Le villi* had been ignored in 1884. Once Ricordi had commissioned the libretto from Verga himself, Puccini visited him at Catania in Sicily to discuss it, also spending some time listening to Sicilian folk music, researching the national costumes, and photographing characteristic locations. He made a quick trip to Malta, but was put temporarily under arrest by the English authorities on suspicion of spying, after he had been seen taking pictures of naval fortifications.

On the voyage home, he made the acquaintance of a fellow traveller, Contessa Blandine Gravina, the daughter of Cosima Wagner by her first marriage to Hans von Bülow, by the expedient of playing excerpts from *Tannhäuser* on the ship's piano, thus prompting her to introduce herself. When he related to her the plot of *La lupa*, she expressed horror at an opera about a *crime passionnel* occurring during a Good Friday procession: 'Lechery and crime, and with a religious procession in it! It would bring nothing but misfortune!' How much this influenced Puccini is not known – though her description would fit the plot of the future *Tosca* equally well. Nevertheless, on his return to Torre del Lago, he wrote to Ricordi: 'Since my return from Sicily and my conversations with Verga, I confess that, instead of feeling inspired by *La lupa*, I am assailed by a thousand doubts which have made me decide to postpone the composition until the play is staged.' In this way, Puccini turned aside from a direct involvement with the *verismo* school, opening the way for his absorption of the best from that movement into his own style of composition, thus taking Italian opera towards the twentieth century and a different form of 'realism', achieved by his unique synthesis of words, music and dramatic action. It is interesting to note how Puccini's concern that his operas should work primarily as staged dramas meant that four of his subsequent operas – *Tosca*, *Madama Butterfly*, *La fanciulla del West* and *Il tabarro* – were based on plays he knew had been successful on the stage. He assured Ricordi in the same letter that he would 'make up for it by plunging into *La bohème*', which he had already been considering as a possible subject. Ricordi replied:

No, I don't wonder that you made the decision that you did, though it saddens me. Again, so many months lost, unfruitful! At least, I see your strong and resolute decision in favour of *Bohème*... Permit me,

56

however, my dear Doge, to observe with my usual frankness that you have been a long time realising that the dialogue in *La lupa* is excessive – after you have begun to set it to music, after the newspapers have already announced the immediate appearance of the opera, after your voyage to Catania! Well, these are useless observations... I wish you a ticket for the most direct train to take you to station *Bohème*.

Henry Mürger (1822-61).

Puccini's choice of Henry Mürger's mainly-autobiographical novel, *Scènes de la vie de bohème*, first published in 1848 and subsequently given as a five-act play, was to lead to considerable controversy. Returning from Turin in March 1893, where he had been supervising the production of *Manon Lescaut*, Puccini mentioned to Leoncavallo that he was working on an adaptation of Mürger's novel. Leoncavallo flew into a rage, arguing that it was he who had originally had the idea of using it. He claimed that he had shown Puccini his libretto the previous winter, and had even offered it to him. This debate was then conducted in public in two rival newspapers, with *Il secolo*, owned by Leoncavallo's publisher Sonzogno, printing an announcement that its champion had been working on *La bohème*. Next day there was a letter from Puccini in *Il corriere della sera*, in which the bitterness that had arisen between the former friends is only too evident:

The declaration made by Maestro Leoncavallo in *Il secolo* yesterday must convince the public that I have acted in perfectly good faith. For it is clear that, if Maestro Leoncavallo, with whom I have been linked for a long time by vivid feelings of friendship, had first told me of what he unexpectedly told me the other evening, I would not have thought of *Bohème* by Mürger. But now – for reasons easy to see – I am no longer willing to oblige him as I would the friend and musician.

For the rest, what does it matter to Maestro Leoncavallo? Let him compose and I shall compose, and the public will judge. Priority in art does not imply that one interprets the same subject with the same ideas. I will only stress that for two months, that is, after the first production of *Manon Lescaut* in Turin, I have been working seriously on this plan and have made no secret of it to anybody.

It is open to question whether Puccini would have been put off a subject because another composer was working on it, yet, wherever the moral right lay, no legal rights of priority were involved. Although Leoncavallo published a letter of reply, and *Il secolo* fired another broadside on his behalf, the friendship was broken and the race was on. In the event, the following November saw Leoncavallo side-tracked into producing *I Medici*, the first in a projected Renaissance trilogy, whereas Puccini's concentration seems to have been sharpened by the conflict, with the result that his version was performed over a year in advance of that of his rival. In fact, Leoncavallo's *La bohème*, given for the first time in May 1897 in Venice, achieved the greater immediate success, but it is the Puccini version that has stood the test of time.

Although they had worked together to rescue the libretto of *Manon Lescaut*, the collaboration of Giacosa, Illica and Puccini really began in earnest with *La bohème*. There is a hint in a letter to Ricordi from Puccini, while he was still in the throes of completing *Manon Lescaut*, that it was Illica, owner of a large library of French literature, who may have suggested the subject to Puccini: 'I talked again with Illica. He has first to finish a comedy, then he will occupy himself with a subject that is *formidable* and *commercial*.' Illica produced a scenario of *La bohème* in five scenes (four acts, since the first act had two scenes – the garret and the Café Momus). In reply, he received an encouraging letter from Giacosa, written just the day after Puccini's letter countering Leoncavallo's claims had been published:

I have read it and admire you. You have been able to extract from a novel, which seems to me exquisite but little suited to the theatre, a real dramatic action. The first acts are stupendous, but I cannot yet visualise the last act, which seems to me very similar to many other acts. But one can find a solution. I very much look forward to a collaboration with you, you nimble and generous spirit.

Things went so well to begin with, that Giacosa was able to tell Ricordi on 31 May 1893 that he had translated Illica's prose text of the first act into verse, sending him a light-hearted poem:

Dolci Ricordi amato,	My Sweet Ricordi,
vi sono molto grato,	I do adore thee,
dell'avermi aspettato	That for me with bated
con animo pacato.	Breath thou hast waited.
Ho sempre lavorato,	How I've worked at it,
ho sempre dibrucato,	To prune and to pat it,
ho sempre tagliuzzato,	To cut and to mend;
ed è un lavoro ingrato.	Yet how thankless the end!
Or mi vedo arrivato	But now let's exult
ad un buon risultato.	At the splendid result.
Puccini ha ormai sicura	Puccini has at last succeeded
trama alle note sue.	In getting all the sleep he needed.
Faremo la lettura	So let me read it to you
domani all'ore due,	Tomorrow on the stroke of two
in Via degli Omenoni.	At Via degli Omenoni.

But within a month, in spite of Ricordi's premature announcement in the *Gazzetta musicale di Milano* that the libretto was complete, Puccini requested Giacosa to revise the projected third act in Musetta's courtyard, in which she throws a party for the Bohemians, while her furniture is being taken away by bailiffs because of her rent arrears. The composer also requested alterations to the scene at the Paris toll-gate, the *Barrière d'Enfer*. Giacosa was soon lamenting to Ricordi that 'the work I'm doing for the libretto is not artistic work, but minute pedantry and most wearisome'. He felt that there was nothing here 'to lift the spirit'. While demonstrating his conscientiousness and goodwill by putting off going to Paris for a performance of his comedy *Tristi amori* – though he could not help drawing Ricordi's attention to his sacrifice – by October he had decided to give up:

In laying down my arms I confess my impotence. The second part of the first act [originally the Latin Quarter scene] presented me with an insuperable difficulty. I do not feel it! I am not inside it. I do not succeed in creating that illusion, that imaginary reality, without which nothing can be achieved. For those few scenes I have wasted more paper and racked my brain more than I have for any of my own plays. For a week now I have been stuck in the scene with the ear-boxing [Musetta and Marcello in Act Three]. I must have re-written it a hundred times, but I have not managed to write a single verse that pleases me... If Puccini were not in such a hurry...then perhaps I could make myself find the strength again... Since I despair of finishing the work in the short time allowed me, and, since it is myself and my insufficiency to which I attribute this shameful surrender,...I take the heroic decision and withdraw from a task which, I am sure, Illica will be able to bring to a happy conclusion alone.

Ricordi, appealing to the good natured Giacosa, eventually managed to persuade him to carry on, though the courtyard scene was soon abandoned altogether, despite strong protests from the librettists. Puccini, by contrast, resisted strong pressure from Illica to cut out the Café Momus, pointing out that he had invented Musetta's scene. At some point during the discussions, this Latin Quarter scene was made into a separate act. For his part, Puccini was not sure that it would be possible to develop the *Barrière* scene in musical terms and suggested that, since it does not itself appear in Mürger, it might be replaced with another scene from the novel. This was successfully opposed by Illica, though he did manage to introduce a scene for the Bohemians at the beginning of the last act to compensate for the loss of the courtyard party.

All this time, Puccini had still been turning over in his mind

Nineteenth-century Parisian café scene.

the possibility of setting *La lupa*, as well as supervising perfor-mances of *Manon Lescaut* in several cities in Europe, so that it was not until July 1894 that he finally abandoned the projected Sicilian opera and began composing *La bohème*. He continued to quibble over details, even demanding the removal of a drinking song and Schaunard's anti-women sentiments, both of which he had originally proposed. This provoked Illica into threatening to withdraw, since he felt 'used, cast aside, taken up again, and once more shoved away like a dog'. Puccini wrote a peevish letter to Ricordi:

I am surprised at Illica's irritation and find it strange. When he came here [Torre del Lago], we were in perfect accord... Now that I go back to him, he chooses to give himself airs. If he says now that I have sent him packing, whose fault is it? All I wanted was that the work should be what it ought to be: logical, terse and well-balanced. But, at the moment, it is none of these things. Must I blindly accept Illica's gospel?... Illica should calm down and then we shall get on with the work. But I, too, want to have my say, as the necessity arises, and I am not prepared to do anybody's bidding.

In his rôle as honest broker, Ricordi brought peace once more and, on 22 August 1894, was writing enthusiastically to Puccini, having received the complete libretto from Illica the previous day. The composer's reply, while still pressing for some details to be removed, expressed considerable pleasure. 'There is no doubt that it is an original work. And how original! The last act is most beautiful. So also is the Latin Quarter, but extremely difficult... The death of Mimi, with all that leads up to it, is very moving.' Ricordi was instrumental in resolving the dispute over the *Barrière* scene, particularly by his valuable suggestion that Musetta should sing the reminiscence of her waltz from inside the inn – namely, off-stage. He continued to press Puccini to keep up the momentum of composition, sending him, in November 1894, these Latin lines:

Toc, toc!	Knock, knock!
Quid petis?	What do you want?
Jacopus Puccinius.	Giacomo Puccini.
Quare?	What for?
Ut videtur si laboret.	To see if he's working.
Laborat.	He is working.
Laborat? ad Bohemian?	On *Bohème*?
Bene est!	That's good!

The Hotel Merciol in the Rue des Canettes, which was once the centre of Bohemian life in Paris.

Puccini continued to work on the opera throughout the following year, making constant requests for changes to the libretto. He was clearly right in feeling that the action would be held up by a quartet, in which the four Bohemians were to propose each other's health, before Musetta arrives bringing with her the seriously-ill Mimi. The librettists did not agree, so, eventually, Puccini cut it by the expedient of having the others shout '*Basta!*' (Enough!) to stop Schaunard as he starts the toast. Giacosa once more tried unsuccessfully to tender his resignation after being requested to intensify the emotion before Mimi dies. 'At the moment when this girl, for whom I have worked so hard, dies,' Puccini wrote to him, 'I should like her to leave the world less for herself and a little more for him who loved her.' Ricordi also managed to deal with Giacosa's repeated complaint – that everyone but he was able to hear Puccini's music – by playing parts of the first two acts to him, and was rewarded by Giacosa's warm reaction: 'Puccini has surpassed all my expectations, and I now understand the reason for his tyranny over verses and accents.'

It was to become the norm for Puccini to spend part of each winter at his Milan flat – 4 Via Giuseppe Verdi, just round the corner from La Scala – where he worked on the orchestration

61

of his operas. In the case of *La bohème* though, he did much of this at Torre del Lago, as well as in Val di Nievole in the Apuan Alps. Here he stayed with a friend, Count Bertolini, on a holiday which he complained made him 'sick and tired', so that he longed for his beloved Torre del Lago. He accepted an invitation for two days shooting at Torre with Count Ginori to 'terrorise my web-footed friends, who have long been panting for my murderous and infallible lead. Boom!' However, despite Ricordi's approval of the expedition, Puccini cancelled it, feeling that he must work instead, though he did take the time to visit Florence with Elvira in order to see Sardou's play *Tosca* with Sarah Bernhardt in the leading rôle. At Torre del Lago, at midnight on 10 December 1895, he finished *La bohème* and, as he later told Fraccaroli, his biographer: 'I had to get up and, standing in the middle of my study, alone in the silence of the night, I began to weep like a child. It was as though I had seen my own child die.'

During the time he had been working on *La bohème* at Torre del Lago, Puccini and a group of friends – a few artists and some villagers – had been meeting to drink, talk and play cards in what was little more than a shed run as a tavern by the local cobbler. Later, when the cobbler emigrated to South America, they bought the shed, and formed the *Club la bohème* with Puccini as honorary president and with the following rules:

1. The members of the *Club la bohème*, faithful interpreters of the spirit in which it was founded, pledge themselves under oath to be well and eat better.
2. Grouches, pedants, weak stomachs, fools, grumblers and other wretches of this kind will not be admitted but will be chased away by the members.
3. The president functions as conciliator in disputes, but pledges himself to hinder the treasurer in the collection of members' subscriptions.
4. The treasurer is empowered to abscond with the funds.
5. The illuminations of the club-room shall be by means of a paraffin lamp. Should there be a shortage of paraffin, the *moccoli* of the members will be used. [A pun – the word means both candle-ends and oaths.]
6. It is forbidden to play cards honestly.
7. Silence is prohibited.
8. Wisdom is not permitted, except in special cases.

Puccini's friends had truly entered into the jocular spirit of his Bohemians as we encounter them in Act One, but the severe Elvira disapproved strongly of the club, particularly when they descended on the house in the evenings to talk and

play cards there in preference to the shed. On such occasions, Giacomo did not participate in the evening's activities, for this was his principal time for work, though he always encouraged people to join him in the study – a habit he shared with Glinka and Scriabin. As he sat at the piano, usually wearing a hat to compose, all he required was that the others ignored him and did not hum or whistle the tunes he was trying out; nothing was more calculated to throw the normally good-natured man into a furious temper. This group of friends nicknamed him '*uomo palla*' ('the human balloon'), because he was inclined to put on weight, so, in 1893, he had been goaded into buying a bicycle on which, Ricordi hoped, he would ride 'from one librettist to another!'

There was much discussion as to where the opera should be first performed. La Scala was now controlled by the publisher Edoardo Sonzogno, to whom the other significant composers of the '*giovane scuola*' were contracted, and he was determined that operas commissioned by the house of Ricordi should not be given there. Puccini was in favour of Rome or Naples, but

63

Ricordi argued successfully for the première to be given in the Teatro Regio, Turin, the scene of *Manon Lescaut*'s triumphant first performance. The management had made alterations to improve the acoustics and stage lighting after earlier objections from the composer. Ricordi warned him 'with my usual frankness' (a phrase he used a great deal in letters to Puccini) not to make excessive demands concerning the cast, reminding him that, as far as success was concerned, it was the opera itself that mattered. Once again, he quoted Verdi as an example to the younger composer, pointing out that the original cast of *Falstaff*, with the exception of Victor Maurel in the title rôle, was 'mediocre', yet Verdi patiently coached them 'day by day, hour by hour ... with that extraordinary patience which finally succeeded in obtaining a performance that was vivacious, lively and persuasive.'

The première was arranged for 1 February 1896, so Illica went to Turin with the composer in the second week of January, leaving Elvira – apparently unwillingly – at Torre del Lago. Puccini wrote to her saying he foresaw 'a great and sensational success', but expressing some doubts about the cast, especially their acting ability. He had hoped the conductor would be Leopoldo Mugnone, but was soon full of admiration for Ricordi's choice, the new musical director at Turin, Arturo Toscanini, who had already conducted performances of *Le villi* and *Manon Lescaut*, boldly introducing the latter to Paris. Toscanini had been born at Parma in 1867 and had studied at the Conservatoire there, beginning his career as a cellist. He had made his mark as a conductor in Rio de Janeiro at the age of 19, when he had directed *Aida* from memory to enormous acclaim, after the orchestra, of which he was a member, had demanded that he replace the regular conductor, who had displeased the audience. Back in Italy at Turin, he had conducted *Edmea* by Catalani – whom he always championed, even naming his daughter Wally after his favourite opera by that composer. In 1892, he directed the première of *Pagliacci* at the Teatro dal Verme in Milan and in December 1895, the Italian première of *Götterdämmerung* at Turin, the first time it was produced separately from *The Ring*. His meeting with Puccini was to lead to a lasting though not always easy friendship, during which he promoted and supported the composer's music, conducting the premières of *La bohème*, *La fanciulla del West* and *Turandot*.

The first night of *La bohème* was only a partial success. The enthusiastic reception given to *Manon Lescaut* was not repeated, though perhaps this was partly due to the fact that Toscanini, never in favour of interrupting the flow of a piece of

Opposite: Arturo Toscanini conducting, drawn by A.I. Keller.

64

music out of respect for its artistic integrity, refused to give in to cries for an encore of Rodolfo's first-act aria 'Che gelida manina' ('Your tiny hand is frozen') and for Puccini to appear on the stage. The second act puzzled the audience with its constantly-shifting episodes that, according to *Il corriere della sera*, lacked 'the cohesion and unity of the first act'. Puccini was given five curtain calls, but the critics were dubious. 'What has pushed Puccini along this deplorable road of *Bohème*?' asked the critic of the *Gazzetta del popolo*, while Carlo Bersczio in *La stampa* advised Puccini to return 'to the straight road of art, persuading himself that this has been a brief deviation.' Not all were so condemnatory. The critic of the Turin newspaper *Fanfulla* felt that his colleagues, after hearing *Götterdämmerung* so recently, were still immersed in the world of 'various mythological divinities' and 'did not know how to leave the world of German transcendentalism in order to hear music which expresses sweet sentiments of the soul and which speaks exquisite melodies of eternal human passions.' Giovanni Pozza in *Il corriere della sera* drew attention to the effective mixture of comedy and pathos, predicting for the opera 'a long future because it pleases no less those who seek in music merely delight than those who make higher demands.' Giacosa and Illica had made this blend possible by basing their

Act III of *La bohème,* as it appeared in the Turin première, depicted by Dante Paolocci in *L'Illustrazione Italiana*, 1896.

66

Contemporary view of Montmartre, Paris.

Mimi on the delicate Francince of Mürger's novel, rather than the coquettish Mimi, thus providing a contrast to the ebullient Musetta.

Mürger himself had succeeded in capturing imaginatively this same blend of comedy and tragedy in the artistic life and atmosphere of Montmartre and the Latin Quarter of the 1840s. Each of his characters is a compilation of several real people from the circle of artists and writers amongst whom he lived. Marcel, for example, is in part drawn from Tabar, a well-known painter who struggled to produce a large historical painting – *The Crossing of the Red Sea*. He was obliged to simplify its scale when the expense of models and costumes grew beyond his means, re-christening the painting *Niobe and her Children Slain by the Arrows of Apollo and Diana* for exhibition in the Salon in 1842. Mürger's Marcel also paints *The Crossing of the Red Sea*, which is rejected by the Louvre jury for five consecutive years. On each occasion, Marcel changes the title until eventually he adds a steamboat, calls it *In Marseilles Harbour* and sells it as the sign for a grocer's shop. Puccini's Marcel is working on a *Crossing of the Red Sea* at the beginning of the opera.

Mürger's original novel appeared in serial form in a literary

67

Ball at the Opera by Edouard Manet; capturing the moment 'as if you looked through a keyhole.' (Degas)

magazine *Le Corsaire*, its fragmentary nature being further emphasised by its title *Scènes*; it is this character that Puccini and his librettists have captured so successfully. This is true not only in the crowded episodes in the second and third acts, but also throughout the opera in the kaleidoscopic variety of the dramatic action and in the often fleeting impressionistic touches of the orchestration. The Italian public was unprepared for this. The critics, for instance, singled out for ridicule the progression of parallel fifths at the beginning of Act Three, yet in an instant they strikingly convey the crackling snow and ice of the dawn at the gate of Paris.

Puccini and his librettists were attempting to do what the French Impressionists were doing in painting. These artists wanted to render onto the 'still plane of the canvas...what meets the eye as it meets the eye' – the impression rather than a 'photographic' reproduction. They had held their first exhibition in 1874 for a largely hostile press and public. While their landscapes increasingly explored the effects of light and air –

remarkable examples of which were Monet's series of paintings of haystacks exhibited in 1891 – the Impressionists were also concerned with contemporary events of little or no significance beyond the fact that they had happened. Mürger, followed by Puccini and his librettists, created a series of 'pictures' of ordinary occurrences in much the same way that Edgar Degas (1834-1917) did of Parisian life. In his paintings and sculptures of ballet dancers, or women ironing, stretching and yawning, or washing themselves in tubs, we see them, as Degas put it, 'as if you looked through a keyhole'. In the same way, in a *Ball at the Opera* Edouard Manet (1832-83) invites us to observe the scene, not as a beautifully framed composition, but as a series of momentary encounters in a crowd. Émile Zola was a great champion of Manet, whom he saw had the ability to translate 'the truths of light and shadow, the reality of objects and human forms into a special language'. Zola revealed that the painter had confessed his love of fashionable society – 'he had an innate need for refinement and elegance'. Yet in this picture Manet reminds us literally that it is merely a slice of life (*uno squarcio di vita* as the Prologue to *Pagliacci* had put it) – we can only see the feet of those on the upper level, while dresses and people are cut off haphazardly by the frame of the painting. What we are presented with is the capturing of a moment around which the world continues oblivious; in the same way, the action profoundly affecting Rodolfo and his friends takes place against the background of busy streets where other people pass by, concerned with their own lives and their own dramas.

The American author, Henry James, in his study.

This is not to say that composer and librettists consciously imitated the Impressionists, although their works were certainly known in Italy; Théodore Duret had published a book on *Les Peintres Impressionistes* in 1878; an Italian painter, Giuseppe de Nittis (1848-84), among others, had visited Paris and come back to Italy inspired by the Impressionists; and it may not be a coincidence that several members of the *Club la bohème* were painters of national renown. For their part, Giacosa and Illica would have been aware of a similar movement in literature, exemplified in the novels of Henry James (1843-1916), an American who visited Europe in search of a tradition in which to write. His early novel *The Europeans* (1878) is a series of sketches, or impressions, reminiscent of Mürger; indeed, one of the main characters is an artist, who is introduced sketching a queue for a horsedrawn omnibus. James's central theme was 'the involvement of art, and what he called generally "the finer consciousness" of a wealthy and ancient culture, in moral corruption and evil [which might be a

69

description of *Tosca*]. To love, to admire, to know, is to be initiated into pain and suffering, and to possess is to partake in tragedy.' It is this latter lesson that the Bohemians learn. To accuse Puccini and his librettists of having produced a light-weight and ephemeral work is to miss how *La bohème* fits into a contemporary European exploration of the importance of the ordinary moment for those who have eyes to see and ears to hear.

After the première, Puccini, as he later confessed to his biographer Fraccaroli, 'returned to my hotel completely heart-broken... I, who put into *Bohème* all my soul and loved it boundlessly and loved its creatures more than I can say... There was in me sadness, melancholy, a wish to cry... I passed a most miserable night. And in the morning I was greeted with the spiteful salute of the critics.' However, the critics were to be confounded by the public; at the end of March, the composer was writing to Ricordi about the 'splendid reception' at Turin, where the opera had been given 24 performances to capacity audiences. The next production, in Rome, met with limited acclaim only. The critic of *Il popolo romano*, Gino Monaldi, singled out Act Two as the least successful because of the undue emphasis on 'realism' in order 'to reproduce upon the stage the sights of the so-called Latin Quarter'. He felt that 'Musetta's *valzer*, the chorus of Parpignol [the toy-seller] and the military music at the end' were praiseworthy, 'but the music of this act, taken altogether, remained nevertheless unequal to the visual aspects of the scene.' After a run in Naples, the opera was presented at Palermo in Sicily, conducted by the man Puccini had suggested for the première, Leopoldo Mugnone. The composer was there to supervise the production and had already begun to make changes to the second act, including the addition of the pink bonnet bought by Rodolfo for Mimì. This prompts a bitter-sweet reflection on the nature of love in the Café Momus later in the act – one of a series of alterations which were soon to improve the act significantly, meeting some of the objections raised by the first critics. Nevertheless, the conductor felt the auspices were not good; the date was Friday 13 April 1896. At first it seemed as though he would be proved right; the oboist was half an hour late and the audience started to jeer and whistle. But he need not have worried: the reception was overwhelming, the curtain calls going on until one in the morning, so that he had to repeat the final scene even though some of the orchestra had already gone home and many of the singers had changed out of their costumes – it is said that Rodolfo did not have his wig on and Ada Giachetti as Mimì had her hair undone.

Within three years, it had been performed all round the

Industrial Manchester, 1876 – 'a horrible place to stay.' (Puccini)

world, in such diverse countries as South America, Egypt, Russia, Spain, Germany, America, Holland, Poland, Greece, France, Malta, Yugoslavia, Turkey, Finland and Algeria. Puccini, accompanied by Giulio Ricordi's son Tito (1865-1932), went to England in April 1897 for the first performance in English, given by the Carl Rosa Company at the Comedy Theatre, Manchester. Neither Tito Ricordi, who had recently joined his father's firm, nor Puccini, spoke English. Herman Klein, music critic of *The Sunday Times*, gave this account of their reactions to the first night:

I never saw two young men in a more despondent frame of mind or more certain of failure. Rehearsals had been going badly and it was impossible that the opera should succeed. However, their doleful anticipations were not to be realised. On the following morning we all travelled back to Euston in a saloon carriage that the railway company had courteously placed at the disposal of the musicians and journalists. We had with us a very different Puccini now – a merry fellow, with a plentiful supply of Italian jokes, and radiant with the recollection of genuine Lancashire feeling.

The great soprano, Nellie Melba, sang Mimi in the first Covent Garden production in Italian in July 1899, though it had been first performed there in English five months after the Manchester production.

In June 1898, Tito Ricordi and Puccini were in Paris for the first French production. The composer had found Manchester a 'land of black smoke, darkness, cold, rain, cotton (but woe to anyone who does not wear wool!) and fog. A veritable inferno! A horrible place to stay!' Although he did come to like Paris, his first impressions of this city were also unfavourable. He wrote to Giulio Ricordi on 15 May: 'I am not in a very happy state here. I should like to be out of here for the sake of my work. I cannot work here. My nerves suffer from too much excitement and I have not the tranquillity which I need. An invitation to a dinner makes me ill for a week; I am not born for a life in *salons* and parties!'

While his dislike of an industrial city like Manchester is understandable, his reaction to fashionable Paris is more surprising. It is revealed most strikingly in a letter of the same month to a chemist in Lucca, Alfredo Caselli:

Nellie Melba as Mimi.

I am sick of Paris. I am panting for the woods with their sweet smells and fragrance; I am panting for the free movement of my belly in wide trousers and with no waistcoat; I pant for the wind that blows, free and fragrant, from the sea; I savour with dilated nostrils the bracing, salty air and inhale it with wide-open lungs! I hate pavements! I hate palaces! I hate capitals! I hate columns! I love the beautiful columns of the poplar and the fir, and the vaults of shady glades where, like a modern Druid, I love to make my temple, my house, my study. I love the green expanse of cool shelters in forest ancient and young. I love the blackbird, the blackcap, the woodpecker! I hate the horse, the cat, the starlings and the lapdog! I hate the steamer, the silk hat, and the dress coat!

He had just written an opera whose very success lay in its exploration of the decadence of the city and its profound effect on individual lives. The characters of *La bohème* live and breathe the city; its contrasts, for example, of bustle and loneliness, fulfilment and hopelessness, joy and despair, riches and poverty, work and unemployment, monotonous grind and artistic endeavour, are re-created beautifully not only in the text but in the music. It is a paradox that the opera could not exist outside the city, yet its creator found it almost impossible to exist within it, and could probably not have written *La bohème* except in the tranquillity of his country retreat at Torre del Lago.

à Nellie Melba, tanto buona
de son ami
P Mascagni

Londra
_17 . 7 . '93 ._

A photograph sent to Nellie Melba by Mascagni, with himself at the keyboard and his composer friends Franchetti and Puccini looking on.

Although he was in tune with the mood of his time, since his operas portray the harsh reality of the world as he found it, yet, at a conscious level at any rate, the man of the country, who wrote operas of the city, appeared to keep the world of his artistic creation and his own experience separate. Those who find in the _Club la bohème_ a connection between the opera and his own life see only the superficial. It is at the subconscious level that the links between his own experience and his operas are to be found, particularly in the Puccini heroine – flawed, adored, doomed. There are further clues in the immediate successors to Manon, Mimi and Musetta – Tosca and Butterfly – as well as in their creator's subsequent private life. These may help explain why Puccini needed to write about such women, and why he remained full of self-doubt and occasional despair in spite of the international fame and recognition he had won with _La bohème_, the opera destined to become the most-performed stage work of all time, whatever the professional critics might say. Perhaps the librettists were prophetic when they made Rodolfo say, as he offers his play to be burnt on the stove to warm them, '_aguzzo l'ingegno_', which might be translated as: 'Genius will out.'

73

Chapter 5

All Life and Fire

I am profoundly convinced that *Tosca* is not a good subject for an opera. (Giuseppe Giacosa in a letter to Giulio Ricordi, 23 August 1896.)

Puccini has a good libretto! Fortunate composer who has that work in his hands! (Verdi about *Tosca*, reported in a letter from Giulio Ricordi to Puccini, 14 October 1896.)

Puccini's visit to Florence with Elvira in 1895 to see a production of Sardou's play *Tosca* was not the only time he had shown interest in it as a possible source. His first librettist, Ferdinando Fontana, had mentioned the play in early 1889

Nineteenth-century view of Florence.

The French novelist, Émile Zola.

after the première of *Edgar*, resulting in an enthusiastic letter dated 7 May 1889 from the composer to his publisher, because he saw in it the possibility of moving away from the 'grand opera' then in vogue: 'I am thinking of *Tosca*. I implore you to take the necessary steps in order to obtain Sardou's permission. If we had to abandon this idea, it would grieve me exceedingly. In this *Tosca* I see the opera which exactly suits me, one without excessive proportions, or decorative spectacle, nor does it demand a superabundance of music.'

For some reason, Puccini expressed no further interest in the subject for six years, during which time he not only wrote *Manon Lescaut* and *La bohème*, but explored other potential subjects. For instance, he went to see the Belgian poet, Maurice Maeterlinck, about his *Pelléas et Mélisande*, though it turned out that it had already been given to Debussy. Zola's novel *La Faute de l'Abbé Mouret* (Abbé Mouret's Peccadillo) (1875) also attracted him, with its sensational story of the love affair between a young priest and a wildly passionate woman, that had been strongly condemned by the Roman Catholic Church. Puccini had met Zola at a dinner given in his honour

75

by the Society of Italian authors, with Giacosa as president, when the French author was visiting Italy in December 1894. Puccini was invited along with Boito and Leoncavallo, but, when he brought up the subject of the novel, it transpired that it had already been promised to Massenet. Another possible idea was a depiction of the last days of Marie Antoinette, originally put forward by Illica, who had previously researched the French Revolution for the libretto of Giordano's opera *Andrea Chénier*. He showed his sketch of some 14 scenes to Puccini, who, having suggested it needed a contrasting revolutionary female character to be sung by a contralto – surprisingly since he otherwise displayed little interest in the voice, then seems to have lost interest in the idea.

Whatever rekindled Puccini's interest in *Tosca*, it was not principally his visit to see it in Florence, since Sarah Bernhardt's 'mechanical' performance caused him to write to Ricordi, questioning whether there was any merit in the play as a source. The publisher replied that he had seen her in the part in Milan in 1889 when she had been magnificent, whereas she had been ill in Florence. This exchange indicates that Ricordi had suggested that the composer should see the play. Certainly he engaged in some double-dealing over the rights to the plot. Several years earlier, the rights to an opera based on Sardou's play had been given to Alberto Franchetti (1860-1942), who had been a fellow-student of Puccini in Lucca, and who had scored modest successes with *Asrael* (1883) and *Cristoforo Colombo* (1892). Illica prepared a libretto and went with Franchetti to discuss it with Sardou in Paris. Verdi was there too, for the first French production of *Otello*, and was at Sardou's house when Illica read his libretto. The 81-year-old composer was so struck by Cavaradossi's farewell to life and art before his execution, that he seized the pages and read it aloud, in a voice overcome with emotion. It was quite probably his reaction that caused Ricordi to realise that this libretto should not be wasted on a minor composer. Puccini obviously agreed, for he immediately demanded that it be made available for him. Ricordi and Illica, according to one story, abandoning their moral principles, persuaded Franchetti that, after further thought, they now felt it was not a suitable subject for an opera, being far too violent and brutal, with an historical background a contemporary audience would not understand. Franchetti is then supposed to have resigned his rights, which were acquired by Puccini within 24 hours. However, Franchetti's heirs later maintained that he had resigned his claim after being persuaded by Ricordi that the subject was much more suited to Puccini. Since the dealings over the

Sarah Bernhardt as Tosca in Sardou's play of the same name.

libretto rights did not lead to a rift between the two composers, as had happened with Leoncavallo over *La bohème*, the latter account is probably more accurate. Certainly, Franchetti was present at the première of Puccini's *Tosca* without any evidence of ill feeling.

With a large amount of the work on adapting the stage work already done by Illica, the dramatisation of *Tosca* caused far fewer problems than *La bohème*. This was also due in part to the tight structure of the original play. Nevertheless, it soon became apparent that Giacosa had a great antipathy to Sardou's play, an opinion shared by many other people. Victorien Sardou (1831-1908) dominated the French theatre for almost 40 years with highly-popular melodramas, largely designed as showpieces for famous actors and actresses, like Sir Henry Irving and Sarah Bernhardt, for whom he had written *La Tosca* in 1887. George Bernard Shaw, a great champion of Ibsen, found Sardou trivial and contrived by comparison, with much of the action happening off-stage, being described and

French dramatist and collector, Victorien Sardou, as portrayed in the December 1880 edition of *Vanity Fair*.

reacted to by those on the stage – a gimmick for which he coined the title 'Sardoodledom'. Sardou was also accused of plagiarism – several writers claimed that the central ideas of *Tosca* had been stolen from their work – but it is hard to know whether Sardou, a skilful weaver of ideas into a convincing tapestry, was guilty of more than working on themes that had parallels elsewhere. For example, the Chevalier Mario Cavaradossi, the painter at the centre of *Tosca*, may well have been drawn from the true story of the poet André Chénier during the French Revolution, which also provided the inspiration for Illica's libretto for Giordano's *Andrea Chénier* (1896). Eugène Scribe's *Adrienne Lecouvreur*, first produced in 1902, as well as being the source for Cilea's opera, probably provided the idea of the unknown woman frequenting a church under the pretext of praying. At any rate, Sardou was able to point his critics to the enormous success his plays achieved, though today he would be virtually unknown were it not for Puccini's opera.

Giacosa's attitude not only stemmed from his low opinion of Sardou's dramatic talents, but from his doubts as to whether *Tosca* was suitable for an opera. On 23 August 1896, he declared in a letter to Ricordi that, whereas with *La bohème* 'the action is of no importance' yet it abounds in 'lyrical and poetic moments', *Tosca* 'is a drama of coarse emotional situations, without poetry':

At a first glance it appears to be suitable because of the rapidity of the dramatic action and the self-evidence of its scenes. And this will the more readily appear to be the case at a first reading of the skilful synthesis, which Illica has made of it. But, the more one studies the action of each scene and tries to extract lyrical and poetic moments, the more convinced one grows of its absolute inadaptability to the musical stage.

Giacosa was writing from his native town of Parella, where he had gone to find the solitude necessary to work on the text in his usual painstaking manner. He offered to resign if the others found that his 'artistic scruples' were holding up progress unacceptably, but, in spite of refusing to accept his resignation, Ricordi was soon pushing the playwright once more to speed up the pace of his work, provoking this response:

I swear to you I am not wasting one hour. But permit me to add that Puccini wastes an infinite number of hours – whether in hunting or fishing, I don't know. I understand very well that a composer cannot start with his work until he has the entire libretto in his hands. But he has in his possession the entire libretto, and two acts of it are in their definitive form. For the third act, he has not only a clear outline of the individual scenes, but also the substance and drift of the dialogue well outlined... To be sure, if he wants the dialogue rendered definitive before he starts to compose, he has only to say so; but, once the dialogue is really definitive, don't let him come afterwards and propose new alterations at every turn.

Indeed, Puccini had not begun composing *Tosca* straight after the first performance of *La bohème* in February 1896. Even after he had started in the summer, his previous opera continued to demand his attention, so that he had to go to Milan for its production at La Scala, to Manchester for the British première, and, in 1898, to Paris for the first French production. When in the French capital, he seized the opportunity to discuss the last act with Sardou, a meeting he later described to Fraccaroli:

That man is prodigious. He was then more than 70, but there was in him the energy and agility of a youngster. Besides, he was an indefatigable and highly interesting conversationalist, talking for hours on end without getting tired. When he touched on an historical subject, he was a water-tap, nay, a fountain; anecdote after anecdote would pour from his lips in a clear and inexhaustible stream. Our sessions simply turned into monologues – most delightful, assuredly, but this did not make for much progress in our *Tosca*. However, he suddenly became compliant and readily agreed with the need to suppress one act and to fuse the scene in the prison cell with that of the execution.

Sardou's five-act play provided Puccini and his librettists with an already taut scenario, which they then skilfully compressed to three acts. The first acts of the play and the opera, set in the church of Sant'Andrea della Valle, are very similar. The opera omits Sardou's Act Two – the reception in the Palazzo Farnese to celebrate Napoleon's defeat of the Austrians at Marengo on 14 June 1800 – by the expedient of placing the celebration cantata, in which Tosca is heard singing off-stage, at the beginning of Puccini's Act Two, set in Scarpia's room in the Palazzo. This scene is the equivalent of Sardou's Act Four, also using some elements of his third act in Cavaradossi's villa where Angelotti is hidden. As Puccini's account explains, Sardou needed some persuading that the two scenes of the play's last act in the Castel Sant'Angelo – the chapel for the condemned and the platform for the executions – could be combined into one scene on the castle platform.

On this occasion, it was to Sardou that Puccini was to

A view of Rome from the River Tiber of the Castel Sant' Angelo, (the setting for Act III of *Tosca*). St Peter's is in the background.

unburden himself of the misgivings and doubts that always assailed him during any composition. Would a French composer not be much more suitable? When the playwright replied that a Roman subject needed an Italian composer, Puccini pointed out that Verdi and Franchetti had both turned it down. Sardou responded that Verdi's interest should be seen as an encouraging sign, since he had only not taken it up because he felt tired with advancing years. 'But my music is tenuous; it is delicate; it is written in a different register... My previous heroines, Manon and Mimi, are different from Tosca,' Puccini replied, only to have this dismissed abruptly. 'It's all the same thing!... Women in love all belong to the same family.' This may say little to Sardou's credit as a dramatist, though his three central characters are more fully sketched than their equivalents in the opera, but Puccini's apprehension seems to have been calmed. Possibly to encourage him, Sardou asked Puccini to play him some of the music intended for the opera on the piano, but, as not a great deal had been composed at that stage, Puccini eked it out by including passages from his two previous operas! The unsuspecting playwright was impressed, and consequently demanded an exorbitant 50,000 francs for the composing rights, though this was eventually toned down to 15 per cent of the gross takings.

In January 1899, they met again to discuss further difficulties

80

with the last act. Tito Ricordi had suggested that Tosca should sing a lament for Cavaradossi before taking her own life. Sardou accepted that, but wanted her 'to swoon and die like a fluttering bird'. This idea was not taken up, however, and the opera ends, like the play, much more effectively when Tosca, having realised that her lover is dead, jumps to her death from the parapet of the castle to escape her pursuers, who have discovered Scarpia's dead body. According to a letter from Puccini to Ricordi, Sardou seems to have been more concerned about the practical details of staging. He had introduced a large flag flying from the top of the castle for a new production of the play for Sarah Bernhardt, which he believed would 'make an enormous effect'. Puccini had a job to persuade him that this was inappropriate for the opera production, since the Italian public would be well aware that the real castle platform, a prominent feature of contemporary Rome, was dominated by an enormous statue of a winged angel. Sardou also drew a sketch for Puccini, which the latter subsequently kept among his curios, showing how he wanted the River Tiber to flow between St Peter's and the Castello. When Puccini observed that it was on the other side, he 'calm as a fish, said: "Oh, that's nothing!"' Puccini summed him up as 'a fine fellow, all life and fire, and full of historico-topopanoramic inexactitudes!'

Concern for such topographical accuracy was a matter of importance to Puccini, particularly in *Tosca*, which, quite exceptionally in opera, is set in three very exact places – the church of Sant'Andrea della Valle, the Palazzo Farnese and the Castel Sant'Angelo, all of which can still be visited in Rome. Puccini's early experience as an organist proved useful when he was working on the first act; there is a distinct ring of truth in the character of the bustling Sacristan, who breaks off his work to say the *Ave Maria*. The composer also took trouble with the liturgical accuracy of the end of the act, when a *Te Deum* is sung to celebrate the news that the Austrians have defeated Napoleon, even though this news is later proved to be incorrect. It is customary for a prayer to be said during the Cardinal's procession to the High Altar before a solemn *Te Deum*. Puccini felt that the usual prayer, *Ecce sacerdos* (Behold the Priest), did not produce the right atmosphere or sound. He wrote to Maestro Vandini at Lucca:

I said I wanted some words to be murmured, therefore I want them. Go to San Martino!... Go to the Bishop!... Go to Father Agrimonti, to Fathers Marianetti, Volpi and Pardini, go to the priests of Antraccoli! Whatever you do, find them, forward them to me. Ask

Caselli, he will be able to find them in some corner of his junkshop... Get the words for me, or I'll become a Protestant. If you don't send me those prayers, I'll compose a 'Funeral March for Religion'... Go to the Bishop!... Tell him to invent something for me. If he does not, I'll write to the Pope and have him thrown out of his job on the grounds of his imbecility.

Vandini failed to respond to such jocularity, so Puccini turned to Father Pietro Panichelli, whom he had met in Rome in 1897, and who was to become a great friend. The Puccinis later nicknamed him '*Pretino*' (little priest) and '*Cappellano di casa Puccini*' (Chaplain to the Puccini household). Puccini requested a prayer that could be murmured 'in subdued and muttered voices, without intonation, precisely as real prayers are said... preferably by the people, because they are more numerous and therefore more effective musically.' It was not, however, Father Panichelli, but Puccini himself who found in an old prayer book the Latin prayer *Adjutorem nostrum in nomine Domini* (Our help is in the name of the Lord), which, with its many open vowel sounds, gave exactly the subdued sound he required.

Nevertheless, Father Panichelli was helpful in several other matters. He sent Puccini the plainsong version of the *Te Deum* used in Roman churches – there being different forms throughout Italy – as well as a detailed description of the Cardinal's procession and the costumes of the Swiss guards.

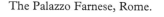
The Palazzo Farnese, Rome.

Furthermore, since the final act begins with the sound of the bells of Rome ringing for the *Ave Maria* before Matins at the beginning of the day, he arranged for Maestro Meluzzi of St Peter's to establish the exact pitch of the largest bell, known as the *campanone*; not an easy task with its myriad of overtones. Puccini then visited Rome and stood on the ramparts of the Castel Sant'Angelo at dawn to hear for himself the Matins bells ring out from Rome's churches. For the same scene, he required a quatrain in the style of a traditional shepherd's song. Through an old Lucchese friend, now a civil servant in Rome, he was able to get the librarian at the Ministry of Education, Luigi Zanazzo, who was also a poet, to write him something that fitted the metre he needed.

Puccini had spent several months of 1898 working on the first act in the isolation of his house at Monsagrati. Here he followed his usual timetable of composition – working in the evening and well into the night, while hunting in the daytime. At this time he was preoccupied with butterflies. Sending some he had caught to his friend Caselli, the chemist in Lucca, he penned a note at two in the morning on 18 August, revealing the customary black mood into which he had fallen during composition: 'These butterflies may serve to give you the idea of the transient character of human miseries. As corpses, let them remind you that, when evening comes, we must all die; while I am racking my brains in the silence of the night to give colour to the Roman heroine, I act as an executioner to these poor frail creatures.'

The second and third acts were completed at Torre del Lago during 1899, but there still remained one major point of disagreement between composer and librettists. On the one hand, Puccini wanted the Farewell to Life and Art, sung by Cavaradossi before his execution, to be a heart-rending expression of the lover's desolation at the prospect of being separated finally from his beloved Tosca. On the other hand, Illica pointed out that Verdi himself had been deeply moved by his verses, and refused to alter them. Although they were clearly well-suited for a Verdian hero to declaim before his death, Puccini knew that he wanted something very different. He therefore wrote some trial words and set them to music, eventually winning the protracted argument by playing and singing them to the librettists, after which Giacosa wrote verses to fit the music. The result was 'E lucevan le stelle' ('The stars are shining'), in which Puccini's simple and touching melodic style expresses most poignantly the lover's absolute despair. Even so, the words do not ring true from a psychological point of view, since Cavaradossi, improbably, reflects on the sexuality of his relationship with Tosca at the moment he faces imminent death. For Puccini, however, the close connection between love and loss was engrained into his consciousness through his experience of life, and it is scarcely surprising that this aria drew from him one of the supreme expressions of *verismo* opera.

Act Three was sent to Ricordi immediately after its completion on 29 September 1899, only to provoke a long letter dated 10 October from the publisher, written, as he confessed, after a sleepless night. He regarded it as 'a grave error of conception and craftsmanship...it would cancel out the splendid effect of Act One...and the overwhelming effect that Act Two is bound to create, which is a true masterpiece of dramatic power and tragic expression.' He complained that the duet between Tosca and Cavaradossi was fragmentary, 'music of a small line that reduces the characters to the stature of pygmies'. To make matters worse, 'one of the most beautiful passages of lyrical poetry – the 'O dolci mani' ['O sweet hands'] – is merely underlined by a scrappy and modest melody which...comes from *Edgar*...stupendous if sung by a peasant woman from the Tyrol, but out of place in the mouths of Tosca and Cavaradossi.' 'Where, in truth,' he asked, 'is the Puccini of that noble, warm and vigorous inspiration?'

Having previously set much store by Ricordi's opinions, in this case the composer replied firmly the next day:

My dear Signor Giulio,
Your letter was an extraordinary surprise to me. I am still suffering from the impact of it. Nevertheless, I am quite convinced that, if you read the act through again, you will change your opinion! This is not vanity on my part. No, it is the conviction of having, to the best of my ability, given life to the drama which was before me. You know how scrupulous I am in interpreting the situation or the words, and how important it is, first of all, to achieve that.

Puccini then argued that the melody from *Edgar* 'emanates from the words', and that the fragmentary nature of the duet was deliberate, because 'Tosca's thoughts continually return to the necessity that Mario's fall should be convincingly simulated'. Acknowledging that this duet had always been the stumbling block, he felt that the librettists had not produced 'anything with any real feeling in it', so that he had had 'to contrive to get to the end without boring the audience too much'. Citing the opinion of the conductor Mugnone and other friends and relatives, who had all formed a favourable impression of it, he offered to come to discuss it with Ricordi, and to alter it, 'if your unfavourable impression persists':

I have always encountered in my dear 'papa Giulio' great delicacy of feeling, not to speak of affection which, you may be sure, is reciprocated in full measure. And I am grateful to you for the interest you take in me, and have always taken, since that day when I had the good fortune first to encounter you. I disagree with you about this third act: it is the first time that we have had a difference of opinion. But I hope, and will go so far as to say I am sure, that you will change your view. We shall see! Toscanini is coming today – and perhaps I shall come back with him tomorrow or the following day. I shall wire you.

The poster for *Tosca* designed by Hohenstein, whose involvement as stage-designer for the première was so controversial.

Whatever discussions took place, no alterations were made, though Ricordi seems to have been fairly accurate in his assessment of the final love duet. It is rather lengthy, in spite of Puccini's concern not to bore the audience; the various elements do not hang together very well; and, though the lyrical section for Cavaradossi, taken from the original version of *Edgar*, has a passionate intensity, it makes the lovers' concluding heroic hymn appear banal and forced.

Because the opera was set in Rome, Illica suggested it should be performed there first, so Ricordi arranged the première for 14 January 1900 in the Teatro Costanzi. The producer was to be his eldest son, Tito. After first studying engineering, he had joined the music publishing firm founded by his great-grandfather. He possessed vision and drive that enabled him, for example, to consolidate the firm's position by establishing branches in several other countries. He was amongst the first in Italy to stress the importance of good acting and effective staging for the success of realistic operas, and took infinite trouble with the details of the first performance of *Tosca*. However, he had little of his father's diplomatic skill and charm, but was authoritarian, uncompromising and short-tempered. His arrogant way of dealing with others made him much disliked, and he even quarrelled regularly with his father, eventually resigning from the firm in 1919. Opera-goers in the capital city were already suspicious of a 'provincial' composer, but when Tito brought in Hohenstein, the stage-designer from La Scala, who had designed the costumes and scenery for Puccini's two previous operas, resentment grew, only to explode when Tito ordered that no outsiders, even critics and relatives of the cast, were to be admitted to rehearsals. Rumours began to circulate that rivals would seek to disrupt the performance, not only by the usual method of hissing, but even by throwing a bomb.

There is a long history in Italy, as well as in many other
countries, of groups being engaged by performers – or the
impresario – to infiltrate the audience in order to influence the
reception of the play or opera by such devices as applause,
calling for encores, and so on. There are records of organised
applauders in early Venetian opera, but such groups could also
be hired to bring down an opera, of which there is a recorded
instance in Bologna as early as 1761. The term *claquer*, for one
who is paid to clap, appears to have been introduced in France,
where a *claque* agency was even opened in 1820. It published

charges for different specialists to form a *claque*, including *tapageurs* who applauded vigorously, *pleurers* who used smelling salts to feign tears of emotion, *connaisseurs* who made knowing exclamations of approval, *bisseurs* who cried 'encore', *commissaires* who spoke well of the performance in the intervals, and *chauffeurs* who 'warmed up' the house before the performance and spoke of the triumph afterwards. In 1919, an actual Italian tariff included: 'applause for a gentleman's entry, 25 lire; for a lady, 15; ordinary applause, 10; insistent applause, 15-17, pro rata; interruptions with *"Bene!"* or *"Bravo!"*, 5; a *"bis"* ["encore"], 50; wild enthusiasm, a special sum to be arranged.' The *capo di claque* was often invited to dress rehearsals and given the score to study.

The cast for *Tosca* was to be headed by Hariclea Darclée in the title rôle, Emilio de Marchi as Cavaradossi and Eugenio Giraldoni as Scarpia, with Leopoldo Mugnone conducting. Some of the singers received anonymous letters before the performance, threatening violence. The rumours of a possible bomb threat had to be taken seriously. In 1894, a bomb was actually thrown backstage, though without loss of life, during a performance of *Otello* conducted by Toscanini in Pisa. Mugnone himself had witnessed the deaths of several people as a result of an anarchist's bomb at a performance he had conducted some years earlier in Barcelona. The fact that Queen Margherita and many politicians were to be present at the *Tosca* première gave further cause for alarm. There was much unrest in Italy at the time, partly as a result of the massive defeat of the Italians at the battle of Adua against Ethiopia in 1896, which brought down the government of Francesco Crispi, formerly Garibaldi's political organiser. But the worsening economy led to industrial riots, the imposition of martial law and considerable loss of life. The Prime Minister of the time, the Marquis di Rudiní, ordered the army into Milan in May 1898 (the *Tatti di Maggio*) and government opponents, both socialists and clerics, were given a total of three thousand years imprisonment by military tribunals. King Umberto, who had succeeded his father, Victor Emanuele II, in 1878, was notorious for his extravagant life-style, which contrasted blatantly with the simple, domestic existence previously led by his father. There had already been two attempts to assassinate him, and, indeed, an anarchist from America was to succeed seven months later at Monza.

Therefore, when a police officer informed Mugnone 15 minutes before curtain-up that a bomb might well be thrown during the performance, and that, if it happened, he should immediately play the National Anthem, it was hardly

The third and successful
attempt to assassinate
King Umberto.

surprising that everyone was on tenterhooks. No sooner had
the performance begun, than whispering and disturbances
could be heard in the auditorium, growing louder until the
singer playing Angelotti and the orchestra were drowned with
shouts of 'Stop! Down with the curtain!' When the curtain did
come down, poor Mugnone rushed backstage in a state of
considerable agitation. Fortunately, it was merely a group of
latecomers trying to get in and the consequent protests of those
already seated; however, it was not an auspicious start. Clearly,
the performers and audience were unsettled, though the opera,
once re-started, was not interrupted again except for encores,
including the summoning of Puccini onto the stage several
times after the encore of 'E lucevan le stelle'.

88

The critics were generally not very complimentary; most took exception to the melodramatic elements of the opera – the torture and the violence – stating that, at times, the libretto 'suffocated' Puccini's artistic creativity. Although sharing this viewpoint, Alfredo Colombani in *Il corriere della sera* pointed out that the composer had grappled successfully in adapting the music to constantly shifting action and the rapid, fragmentary dialogue. *Il corriere d'Italia* used the whole front page spread to discuss the opera and, though it congratulated the composer, it felt he should not 'have attempted something the futility of which ought not to have escaped him'. Perhaps deciding that he had better distance himself from this apparent failure, Illica wrote a strong letter to Ricordi complaining that the libretto was:

so mutilated and anti-musical that it must be considered just the shadow, the outline of the libretto, which had so enraptured Giulio Ricordi. For these reasons, and for others of which you are certainly

The Royal Opera House, Covent Garden, 1896.

89

Working-class children queuing for free meals in turn-of-the century London.

aware, I am sure that you will not be surprised if, since it seems questionable whether my humble work would, or would not, be acceptable, I take my leave of you, dear Signor Giulio – taking with me, however, together with my present sorrow, precious memories of the affectionate kindnesses of the unforgettable days long past.

Puccini was beginning to resign himself to the fact that *Tosca* was a failure, when it became obvious that the public took a very different view. After 20 more performances to full houses in Rome, it was given successfully in several other Italian cities. *Tosca* was soon being performed in many countries round the world and was translated into a bewildering variety of languages. Covent Garden put it on in Italian in July 1900, only six months after its première. Puccini came to London for this production, also seeing a performance of *La bohème*. He was entertained by the Rothschilds, but he wrote to Elvira: 'I have had enough of London. It is cold here, quite like autumn... London would be a better and more interesting place to stay in than Paris. It is the language difficulty which is

Interior scene of The Savoy Hotel, London, around 1900.

The singer Antonio Scotti as Scarpia in his dressing room between acts.

so depressing. I don't understand a syllable of it. Well, I know the numerals (the first ten) and some addresses to which I can go in a cab!' With such a limited command of English, it was difficult for him to appreciate a play he was taken to see, *Madame Butterfly*, but, even so, the story of the Japanese geisha girl betrayed by an American sailor touched him.

During his visit, he was shown both sides of London life, as he related in another letter to Elvira: 'We went to see the slums of London, which interested me very much. I am almost always invited out, tonight also. I went to dine with some friends at Maxime's, where there were plenty of *cocottes*. What elegance and what beauties! But afterwards we went home, quietly, quietly, like good boys.'

He felt that the singers for the Covent Garden production were better than at La Scala. Milka Ternina created a great impression in the title rôle ('a true creation' in the composer's judgment), Cavaradossi was Fernando de Lucia, while Antonio Scotti, who was to make the part very much his own for the next 33 years, played Scarpia for the first time. Puccini noted: 'Scotti marvellous; bad voice, but talent, and of great stature in the part.' Although some critics objected to the torture scene, the opera was enthusiastically received. Ternina and Scotti both took part in the first production at the Metropolitan Opera, New York, in February 1901 where again critical reaction was cool, in contrast to the popular acclaim of the audiences.

The critic of *L'avanti* had voiced the general feeling of much initial critical opinion of *Tosca* by focusing on the apparent unsuitability of the libretto for the composer's temperament. Yet many had praised the music. Alessandro Parisotti in *Il popolo Romano* had found that 'the gentle lyrical passages, coming between the dark and sadly heavy colours of the drama, almost always win out, creating music of beauty and durability.' The striking drama took many by surprise – 'events follow one another, almost tumultuously, and the music cannot afford to linger,' as Colombani put it. Time was needed, as Eugenio Cheechi pointed out in *Nuova fanfulla*, to gain a greater appreciation of the largely successful way in which Puccini's music swept the audience into the very heart of a drama, albeit a melodrama, that captured and held their imagination. Puccini was to write greater music, but in *Tosca* he had created an opera that was quick to gain a prominent and secure place in the world's operatic repertoire, a position it has retained ever since.

Chapter 6

Fiasco at La Scala

Butterfly, Diabetic Opera, Result of an Accident. (Newspaper head-line, 18 February 1904 [the morning after the première].)

Butterfly remains...the most heartfelt, and most expressive opera that I have conceived. (Puccini, in a letter to Camillo Bondi on the same day.)

It is uncertain who suggested to Puccini that, while he was in London in 1900 for the production of *Tosca*, he should go to see David Belasco's one-act play *Madame Butterfly* at the Duke of York's Theatre, where it was being given with Jerome K. Jerome's *Miss Nobbs*. William Boosey, the music publisher, later claimed the credit in his autobiography, but it was more likely to have been the manager of Covent Garden, Frank Nielson, or Alfredo and Maria Angeli, Puccini's London friends. The fact that the composer understood little of the dialogue was probably an advantage, since it was, at times, fairly excruciating. Butterfly says, after Pinkerton has left: 'W'en he goin' 'way, he say in tha's doors: "Madam Butterfly, I have had ver' nice times with my Japanese sweets [sic] heart, so now I goin' back to my own country and here's moaney [sic] – an' don' worry 'bout me – I come back w'en robins nes' again!"' As she dies in his arms at the end, she whispers: 'Too bad those robins didn' nes' again.' Nevertheless, it had caused a sensation in New York, and was well received in London, where Belasco brought it seven weeks later. He told his biographer that:

after the curtain fell [Puccini] came behind the scene to embrace me enthusiastically, and begged me to let him use *Madame Butterfly* as an opera libretto. I agreed at once, and told him he could do anything he liked with the play, and make any sort of contract he liked, because it is not possible to discuss business arrangements with an impulsive Italian, who has tears in his eyes and both arms around your neck.

This colourful reminiscence is not borne out by the facts. Not only does it not sound at all like the reserved composer, but, on his return to Italy, Puccini toyed with a great many other possible subjects. He raised again the question of *Pelléas et Mélisande* or *La Faute de l'Abbé Mouret*, both of which he already knew were not available to him; so, far from being convinced about *Butterfly*, he was obviously testing every possibility. Several novels were considered and rejected as possible subjects, including Dostoyevsky's *Memoirs from the House of the Dead* – which later formed the basis for Janáček's *From the House of the Dead* – Victor Hugo's *Les Misérables* and Rostand's *Cyrano de Bergerac*. Ricordi re-opened the idea of an opera about the French Revolution, and even commissioned Illica to write a scenario for *Marie Antoinette*, but again failed to tempt the composer.

As at other points in his career, Puccini considered a collaboration with Italy's most distinguished poet, Gabriele D'Annunzio. In July 1894, writing to the composer and author, Carlo Clausetti, who later became Ricordi's manager, and who had originally suggested the co-operation, Puccini commented: 'For years and years, it had been my idea to obtain something original and tender from Italy's first talent. Explain to him my kind of style – poetry and again poetry, tenderness mixed with pain, sensuality, a drama surprising and burning, and a rocketing finale.' As he had sensed, however, their creative styles were too far apart, and there was the added difficulty that D'Annunzio made excessive financial demands. In August 1906, a letter from D'Annunzio to Camillo Bondi gives the poet's perspective: 'My contacts with the Maestro from Lucca have been sterile. He is overwhelmed by the power of Poetry. Two excellent outlines – *Parisiana* and the *Rose of Cyprus* – seemed too grandiose for him. He went so far as to confess to me that he needs a "small, light thing to be put to music in a few months, between one trip and another". For this he came to the poet of *Francesca da Rimini*!' Though they subsequently kept in touch, nothing transpired, so that by November 1918, Puccini was writing to Clausetti: 'Everything you say, I foresaw and felt long ago. The Poet has little feeling for the lyrical theatre. Pass it in review and you will see that I am right. He always lacked the sense of true, pure and simple humanity. Everything is always a paroxysm, a tightly drawn cord, an excess of expression.'

Of all the many subjects he considered at this time, it was the splendid comic novel by Alphonse Daudet *Tartarin de Tarascon*, about a Provençal Don Quixote, that most attracted him. Although he had doubts about whether it would seem too

The Italian poet Gabriele D'Annunzio, in a photograph taken in 1914.

much like Verdi's *Falstaff*, the thought of a comedy more in the mode of *La bohème* was clearly exciting to him after the reception of *Tosca*. This can be seen in his description of the proposed final scene in a letter to Illica:

...A large square with oleander trees of diverse colours, white houses in the style of those of Palermo and Malta, the sky a dark cobalt blue, sun, a large practicable bridge over the Rhône in the background. A big Farandole with chorus, who come running ahead of Tartarin and his Tarascon, March. Groups of singing and shouting villagers... All this with much gaiety and with the impetuosity of the southern French – orchestra, chorus, bands [on the stage] and bells – in short, a rapid and fulminant scene. It will consist of one musical number, and the close must be gay, warm-hearted, radiant, rich and clamorous. We shall make this opera an original, diverting and youthful work!

Nevertheless, Giacosa withdrew from the project, and Illica, rather more keen on pushing a satire by himself set in the Milan of the eighteenth century, was not co-operative. As it turned out, the rights were not available, so the project foundered, though Puccini did consider the idea again five years later, only to give it up because he became convinced finally that Tartarin was too similar to Falstaff.

The failure to settle on a subject brought a string of complaints from Puccini about his enforced inactivity. A month after the *Tosca* première, he wrote to Elvira that he was 'sick to death of being *inoperaio*' (a pun on being out of work and without an opera), using the same play on words in a letter to Ricordi in the following August to describe himself as 'one of your unemployed workmen'. Significantly, in that letter he asked Ricordi whether he had written to New York 'for that American subject'. In November, he wrote that 'among the thousand suggestions, which have rained upon me, I have found nothing which suits me', although he had looked seriously at Benjamin Constant's *Adolphe*, which he found 'very poor material indeed' and too similar to *La traviata*. Again he railed: 'I have not yet found *my* subject. I despair of it and am tormented in spirit. If, at least, some reply would come from New York.' This was, of course, a reference to *Butterfly*, but Ricordi's agent was finding it difficult to reach agreement with Belasco – so much for the author's later account that he had given Puccini *carte blanche*!

In many photographs taken of David Belasco he is wearing clerical dress, probably in imitation of Liszt; yet he was, in reality, a Portuguese Jew, whose family had emigrated to San Francisco from England during the Gold Rush. He was

The dramatist David Belasco.

educated by Catholic monks in British Columbia, which no doubt influenced his later choice of dress, though he escaped from the monastery to join a travelling circus as a clown, later becoming an itinerant actor. However, it was as a producer that he made his mark, insisting on natural acting, and introducing realistic scenery and effects that were important in the development of the American Theatre. For instance, his production of his own *Madame Butterfly* began with illuminated backdrops of rice-fields, cherry blossom in a garden, fishing boats and a snow-capped volcano. Butterfly's night vigil of 12 hours lasted for 14 minutes on stage with not a word spoken – night fell, stars appeared, the lanterns to celebrate her husband's return went out one by one, dawn broke, birds sang – it was hailed as the masterpiece of one who was called 'the wizard of the stage'. Belasco's plays were modelled on Sardou, and, like the French author, he was accused of, and even sued for, plagiarism. As an example, his *The Darling of the Gods* contains a scene remarkably similar to Scarpia's use of the torture of Cavaradossi to extract information from Tosca.

Belasco had taken the subject of *Butterfly* from a story by John Luther Long in the American *Century Magazine* in 1898, about a geisha and her child abandoned by the American naval-officer father. Long claimed that it was based on the true story of Tsuru Yamamura, who had a son by an English merchant. When he left her, she unsuccessfully tried to commit suicide, so he took their child to live with him in Nagasaki, where the boy became the pupil of Long's nephew. There are other accounts about the origin of the story, but it was clearly based on fact. Long, a lawyer in Philadelphia, got much of the local colour from his sister, the wife of an American missionary in Nagasaki, as well as from the widely-read novel by a French naval officer, Pierre Loti, *Madame Chrysanthème*, which contained detailed descriptions of the Japanese people, their homes and their character.

Loti's novel, first published in 1887, was part of a growing awareness of Japan, that had been fuelled by articles, magazines, books, plays and even operas. An Irish journalist, Lafcadio Hearn, went to live in Japan, married a Japanese woman, and became a Japanese citizen, changing his name to Koizumi Yakumo. From 1890 to his death in 1905, Hearn wrote innumerable articles and books, culminating in *Japan: an Attempt at an Interpretation* (1904). His writings, translated into several European languages, along with those of the De Goncourt brothers in France, and of Ernest Fenollosa, an American professor of art and philosophy, further excited interest in a land that had been virtually unknown until that time. In 1853, Commodore Perry of the US Navy had sailed into Tokyo harbour at the head of a powerful squadron, demanding free entry to the port, which was granted the next year, following pressure from the USA, Britain, France and Russia. This ended 300 years of self-imposed isolation, during which only the Dutch East India Company and China were able to enter and trade with Japan – the Dutch had a small trading colony on Deshima island off the coast of Nagaski. From 1854, trade agreements between Japan and other countries were made, the ensuing flood of art works to Europe sparking off a craze for things Japanese.

The interest of Western artists was aroused in the art and culture of this distant land, whose customs and view of life seemed so tantalisingly different. The Japanese style of composition and vigorous framing, for example, had a marked influence on the French Impressionists – Vincent Van Gogh, Émile Bernard and Paul Gauguin, in particular. Cloisonism with its dark outlines filled with flat elementary colours like Japanese woodcuts is the most obvious, though by no means the only, result. Van Gogh owned many Japanese prints, including some by Utagawa Hiroshige (1797-1858). In the middle of the nineteenth century, as Japan was moving into its modern period and opening itself to the outside world, Hiroshige embarked on his largest and final series of prints, *A Hundred Views of Famous Places in Edo* (as Tokyo was then called). Van Gogh painted his own version of *Shower of Rain on the Ohashi Bridge*, as well as many other paintings influenced by Japanese art. He wrote to his brother Theo on 24 September 1888: 'I envy the Japanese the extreme clarity, which everything has in their work. It is never tedious and never seems to have been done in haste. Their work is as simple as breathing, and they do a figure in a few sure strokes with the same simple ease that you button your coat.' He attempted to establish an artistic community in the yellow house at Arles, modelled on life in a Japanese monastery. Just before he left for Arles in 1888, he wrote: 'As regards living in the south, even if it is more expensive, look, we love Japanese painting, we are influenced by it – all Impressionists have that in common – and would we not be going to Japan, that is to say the equivalent of Japan, the Midi?' Once in Arles, he wrote: 'The weather here stays fine, and, if it was always like this, it would be better than the painters' paradise; it would be Japan utterly.' He sent a self-portrait of himself as a *bonze* (a Japanese priest) to Paul Gauguin as an invitation to join him in the yellow house. 'I conceived it as the portrait of a *bonze*, a simple worshipper of the eternal Buddha. I wanted my portrait to convey myself and an impressionist in general.' In the end, the two quarrelled; Van Gogh threatened Gauguin with a knife, then cut his own ear off, thus ending his dream of a Japanese-style community.

In opera, Gilbert and Sullivan's *The Mikado* (1885), to which Puccini was to refer, Messager's *Madame Chrysanthème* (1893) and Mascagni's *Iris* (1898) had all explored Japanese themes, though, perhaps even more significantly, two earlier operas were based on the story of a non-white woman who falls in love with a white man and then commits suicide after he deserts her – Meyerbeer's *L'Africaine* (1865) and *Lakmé* by Delibes (1883).

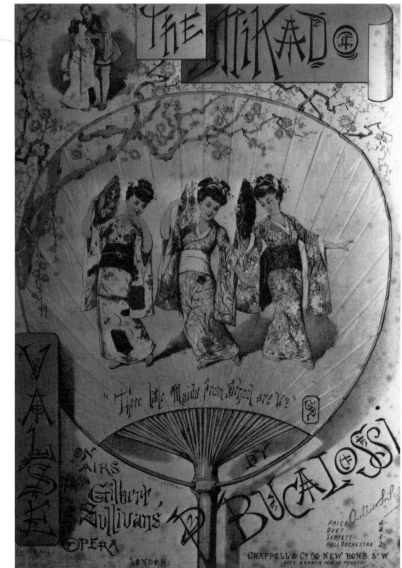

Cover to a selection of music from Gilbert and Sullivan's opera *The Mikado*.

Throughout 1900, while Puccini was waiting to begin working seriously on *Butterfly*, he kept an eye on new productions of his other operas. Puccini premières at Lucca were now very special events, and that for *Tosca* was no exception. The composer was given 27 curtain calls by an audience that included Eleonora Duse and Gabriele D'Annunzio, and was presented with a bust of himself by Giuseppe Bianchi, paid for by public subscription. He also went to Brussels for a performance of *La bohème* and to Bologna for *Tosca* at the Teatro Communale with Ada Giachetti and Enrico Caruso (1873-1921). They had first met in 1897, when singing together in *La bohème* at Leghorn in 1897, the year that Caruso scored his first major success in *La Gioconda* at Palermo, followed by an appearance in the première of Cilea's *L'arlesiana* at the Teatro Lirico in Milan. Giachetti left her husband for Caruso and they lived together until she left him 11 years later. They had four children, two of whom survived: Rodolfo, nicknamed Fofò, and Enrico Jr, nicknamed Mimmi [sic] after Puccini. After the Bologna performance, Puccini said he had never heard Cavaradossi better sung. Caruso was to maintain that he had been offered the chance to create the rôle at the Rome première, and that no explanation had ever been given for the withdrawal of the offer. Nevertheless, composer and singer became firm friends.

In December of the same year (1900), Caruso made his début at La Scala in *La bohème*. It was a disaster, or, in the words of the general manager, Giulio Gatti-Casazza, 'not lucky'. The tenor had laryngitis, but did not tell anyone, so each aria was greeted with stony silence. Puccini could not bear to stay to the end. However, the infection soon cleared up, and Caruso became a huge success in Milan, particularly in *L'elisir d'amore*. A measure of his increasing fame was his selection as one of the singers to take part in the memorial concert for Giuseppe Verdi, who died at the age of 87 on 27 January 1901. Puccini, Leoncavallo, Mascagni and other representatives of the Italian musical world attended the simple funeral he had requested as well as the concert at La Scala conducted by Toscanini, in which Caruso sang the Duke's part in the *Rigoletto* quartet. A month later, in accordance with the great composer's last wishes, he and his wife, Giuseppina, were re-buried in the newly-completed oratory at the Casa di Riposa (the Musicians' Rest Home he had founded). Puccini, representing Lucca, joined others from every sphere of Italian life to walk behind the coffin through the streets of Milan, which were packed by two hundred thousand people. 'With him the purest and most luminous glory of Italy was extinguished',

The celebrated tenor, Enrico
Caruso.

Puccini wrote. 'For the true greatness of our country, let us
hope that the virtues of the man and the artist will be imitated
and carried on.' It is doubtful whether the two composers ever
met. Verdi preferred the music of Mascagni, whereas Puccini,
though he admired *Falstaff*, often said that he preferred
Wagner, especially *Parsifal* and *Die Meistersinger*. He wrote a
brief *Requiem* for chorus and organ in memory of Verdi some
four years later, but it was never published.

The contract with Belasco was finally agreed in April 1901,
although Puccini had already sent Illica a translation of Long's
original story. Reaching agreement about the libretto proved
much easier than with *La bohème*, but there were still major
points of dissension between the three collaborators. The principal one was over the number of acts. Puccini originally envis-
aged 'two quite long acts', so Illica sketched a plan for a
prologue of the wedding of Pinkerton and Cio-Cio-San (nick-

Illustration to the original story *Madam Butterfly* by John Luther Long.

named Butterfly), followed by three scenes, the middle one of which would be set in the American Consulate, the others in Butterfly's house. The prologue was soon expanded into Act One, and the first scene of the second act became an act in its own right. Long's story ended with Suzuki, the maid, saving Cio-Cio-San from her attempted suicide, whereas Belasco's play ended with her death. Although Illica favoured Long's ending, Puccini insisted on following Belasco. Such changes caused enormous frustration for Illica and Giacosa, and certainly contributed to the other main source of friction, Giacosa's slow speed of working. Illica was, nevertheless, optimistic and felt that the librettists could surpass Belasco, given the support of composer and publisher, to whom he wrote:

Butterfly is the strongest plot Puccini has ever had, strong and new,

100

East meets West –
traditional costumes and
posture in a Japanese railway
carriage in 1909.

but not easy. We must find a way to have mutually beneficial confer-
ences, as we had for *Bohème*. I said strong and new, and, I would also
add, the most suited to Puccini's elegance...even without Belasco.
And our self-esteem would lead us to work wonders!

Meanwhile, other problems loomed. Giacosa was not well;
yet he was trying to write another libretto while taking the
waters at Salsomaggiore in the summer of 1901. Then he was
further distracted by his attempts to patch up a scandal after
his son had been involved in a duel. Puccini became very impa-
tient, but eventually he received the first act. In the spring,
acting on a suggestion by Illica, Puccini met the Japanese
actress, Sada Jacco, when she was in Milan as part of a
European tour. This gave him the chance not only to question
her, through an interpreter, about Japanese customs, but to

101

hear the high pitch and rapid delivery of the Japanese female voice. He also had several sessions with Madame Ohyama, the wife of the Japanese ambassador, who told him 'a great many interesting things and sang [him] some native songs'. Although she criticised the choice of names for several of the characters, especially Prince Yamadori, which she felt was a name more suited to a woman, Puccini did not take her advice on this. However, he seriously pursued other avenues of research into Japanese life and customs, consulting a wide variety of books and listening to gramophone records of Japanese music.

As he progressed with the composition, Puccini realised that the three-act structure did not work, as he explained to Ricordi in a letter dated 16 November 1902:

For two days I have been in my worst humour, and do you know why? Because the libretto, as it stands, is no good after the end of the second act. The realisation of this has distressed me very much. But now I am convinced that the opera must be in two acts! Don't get frightened!

The Consulate was a grave error. The drama must move to its close without interruption – rapid, effective, terrible! In planning the opera in three acts, we were making for certain disaster. You will see, dear Signor Giulio, that I am right.

Ricordi needed some convincing, particularly because this would make the second act very long. Although Illica had felt that the Consulate act provided a good Western contrast to the Japanese setting, he was prepared to accept that Puccini was probably right in insisting on the unity of place for the drama – though the length of Act Two certainly contributed to the initial hostile reception it was to receive. Giacosa was not so easy to budge. Puccini visited him in January 1903, and then wrote him a pleading letter: 'Everything crumbles! What is now to become of poor *Butterfly*, into which I am putting so much of myself?!' Giacosa's reply, dated 17 January, indicates clearly how he predicted the disaster that was to overtake the opera:

I too feel grieved, and profoundly so, at our dissent. I have worked on this libretto with more love than I put into the other two, and was satisfied with my work... I am convinced – and the more I ponder it, the more convinced I become – that the curtain ought to fall between the futile night vigil and Pinkerton's reappearance... I am convinced that the result of fusing the second with the third act would be, musically, an act which would be interminable and too contrived... To sum up, the sketch which you brought me appears to me absurd, and I foresee (however splendid the music) a disaster with the public. And, for that, I will assume no responsibility whatsoever... Seeing that there is such an absolute divergence of views between us, I must cease meddling further.

The opera, as we know it today, has a long second act in two parts, which some productions treat as two acts with an interval between. Although he may have been justified in his complaints, Giacosa was persuaded once again to retract his resignation. All seemed clear for the work of composition and orchestration to move rapidly ahead.

It was not to be. Having been suffering from a throat complaint, exacerbated by his smoking, Puccini decided to consult a specialist in Lucca on 25 February 1903. Afterwards, the Puccinis (Giacomo, Elvira and Tonio) dined with several old friends, including the chemist Alfredo Caselli at Rebecchino, one of Lucca's oldest restaurants. Caselli tried to persuade them to stay overnight as it was foggy and frosty. However, Puccini was keen to return to Torre to carry on working on *Butterfly*. They set out in his brand new automobile – he had become captivated by cars, as he had been by motor-boats, and was the first person in Torre to own one. It was driven by their young chauffeur, Guido Barsuglia, but, only a few miles from Lucca, the car skidded on a bend after a small bridge and plunged into a field some 15 feet below. Luckily, a doctor lived nearby and, hearing the unusual sound of a car, had been looking out at the time. Elvira and Tonio were only shocked, but the chauffeur, flung out of the car, which was now upside down, had a broken thigh. Puccini was nowhere to be seen, and it was assumed he had also been thrown from the car. After a frantic search, he was discovered unconscious underneath the car, almost asphyxiated by petrol fumes. He had been miraculously saved from being crushed to death by a fallen tree trunk, on which the car was resting. He was taken to the doctor's house where his broken right shin was unfortunately set so badly that it had later to be re-broken and re-set, leaving him with a permanent limp. After the wound refused to heal, further investigations revealed that he had diabetes.

Thus began eight months of pain, boredom and frustration for the composer. To begin with, he could not work at all. In March, the temporary bandages were replaced by a cast. 'I am all plaster-cast,' he wrote to a friend, 'my legs are emaciated, without flesh, and they have put me on a diet of five meals a day with strychnine and Karlsbad water.' He received more than 300 cables, including one from the King, from Sardou in Paris, and Mascagni in San Francisco. These were followed by a vast number of letters from all round the world, and countless visitors. He was able to move around in a wheelchair – he

103

called it his 'automobile without fuel' – but he was told in May that it would be at least three months before he could put his foot on the floor. Like Wagner, Puccini composed at the piano, so this was a bitter blow. 'Farewell to everything, farewell to *Butterfly*, farewell to my life!', he wrote in a letter to Illica. 'I am now really completely discouraged.' By this time, his flow of visitors had diminished, and he begged Caselli to come to stay with him: 'I am alone with my eternal boredom and sadness. Nothing interests me. Even the tepid springtime irritates me. I feel I am in prison, constantly guarded and watched.'

The 'guard' consisted of Elvira, her sister, Ida, and Puccini's sister, Nitteti – Fosca was now married and living in Milan, and Tonio was at school in Switzerland. Not only was Puccini dependent on their ministrations, but he was unsure of the motivation behind their close attention. Certainly Ricordi was aware that Puccini had been engaged in a liaison with a woman from Turin, whom he had met on a train. Little is known about her, except that she was a law student whose christian name was Corinna, though others referred to her as 'the Piemontese' [the woman from Piedmont]. Ricordi suspected, incorrectly, that a venereal disease was contributing to the composer's slow recovery. The publisher wrote to him on 31 May urging him to keep his promise, already given, to mend his ways:

Is it at all possible that a man like Puccini, that an artist who moves millions of people and makes them cry with the power and spell of his creation, can become a ridiculous and ugly toy in the meretricious hands of a vulgar and contemptible woman?... Does this man no longer possess the faculty of clear judgment?... And does this man not realise the immense distance that separates love from repellent obscenity, which destroys in a man his moral personality and physical vigour?

Ricordi had a great many harsh things to say about the woman, 'who gets him under her thumb and, like a foul vampire, sucks his mind, blood and life,' which Puccini refuted in his reply. There was clearly an orchestrated campaign to separate Giacomo and Corinna, which involved not only Elvira's friends and relations, but also Puccini's sisters, particularly Ramelde who was in touch with Illica about it. He advised her that 'a return to the Piemontese could be very dangerous for him, because it seems certain that she, if the affair began again, would realise how easily the fish was able to get away [from Elvira] and would start thinking things over, working out a way to prepare a net that would entrap the fish, no matter what he wished.' The accident provided the opportunity for the

104

interested parties to manoeuvre the composer into ending the affaire, which included financial compensation for Corinna.

In June, the doctors were able to provide a steel brace that enabled Puccini to sit in some fashion at the piano. In August, Giacomo and Elvira escaped the summer heat by going to Boscolungo in the Apennines for a period of convalescence. He became 'fat and flourishing again like a chaffinch', as he told Ricordi, though walking with great difficulty on two sticks – it was to be three years before he was able to walk without a stick. He finished the celebrated *intermezzo* in August, telling Ricordi that he thought it good, and that it would not be long until the opera was finished.

After completing the orchestration of Act One in September, he spent some time in Paris, where, as the composer of *La bohème*, he was fêted everywhere as a great celebrity. He and Elvira had gone for the première of *Tosca* at the Opéra-Comique, where the music director was André Messager, whose operetta *Madame Chrysanthème* (1893) had been the first musical exploration of Pierre Loti's story. After its failure, he had retired to Maidenhead in Berkshire, but the success of his *Les p'tites Michu* in 1897 had brought him the Paris appointment. He did much to introduce Wagner's music to France, as well as championing Mozart, Charpentier and Russian music. He was responsible too for the first production of *Pelléas et Mélisande* (which is dedicated to him), and reviving interest in Gluck and Rameau. He worked with Puccini on the score of *Tosca*, while Sardou took charge of the dramatic action. The première was, according to Puccini, 'a veritable triumph... Italian-style with shouts and calls for encores.' The critics, while acknowledging its popularity, were less kind. 'The opera is coarsely puerile, pretentious and vapid', decided *Le Mercure de France*, and Gabriel Fauré in *Le Figaro* said it had 'disconcerting vulgarities'. But all the performances were sold out – the public loved it.

During this visit, he heard *Pelléas et Mélisande* and met Claude Debussy. Although Puccini noted that it contained not one aria, he admired the orchestration, which was to influence his own. Debussy wrote of *La bohème* in *Gil Blas* in February 1903: 'Even if Monsieur Puccini is attempting to recapture the atmosphere of the streets and people of Paris, it is still an Italian noise he makes. Now I wouldn't hold the fact of his being Italian against him, but why the devil choose *La bohème*?' Debussy was much influenced by oriental music. He was regarded as the founder of the Impressionist School in music, which replaced the conventional, formal structures of Romanticism with music that was delicate and sensitive, even

The French composer
Claude Debussy, whose
orchestration Puccini
admired greatly.

voluptuous, suggesting meaning, rather than stating it. He was
a friend of the poet Mallarmé, who, with Baudelaire, Verlaine
and others, was working along similar lines in poetry. 'To name
an object,' Mallarmé wrote, 'is to sacrifice three-quarters of the
enjoyment of the poem, which comes from the guessing bit by
bit. To *suggest* it – that is our dream.' Debussy, with his oriental
melodies, backed up by harmonies based on Eastern-sounding
scales and shimmering orchestration, successfully translated
into a European idiom elements of this new exotic world that
had so captivated him. Puccini's attempts to convey the
Japanese atmosphere, on the other hand, may well have been
partly responsible for the hostile reception of the original
version of *Madama Butterfly*. Although he successfully incorporated authentic Japanese tunes into the music, he also experi-
mented with devices of harmony, rhythm, orchestration, and

106

the use of the pentatonic (five-tone) scale, to make those sections of the opera where the focus is on the Japanese characters sound convincingly exotic to his Western audience. No doubt, at first hearing, much of it sounded strange and unappealing, although, later, critics and audiences alike were to recognise that, however 'Eastern' the music appeared, it still bore the unmistakable stamp of Puccini.

Back at Torre, he completed the opera at 11.10 pm, two days after Christmas. Even with the accident, it had only taken three years. One further dispute arose, this time between Ricordi and Giacosa, who tried to insist that verses which he had written for Pinkerton in the last act, but which Puccini had not set to music, should be included in the printed libretto. A protracted correspondence ensued, until in January, with Giacosa ill, Ricordi wrote to him words, which, though in jest, had a prophetic ring: 'It's time to end this! Either you get well or there will be war to the death between us.' As always, Giacosa conceded defeat, and was soon heavily involved in preparations for the première at La Scala, writing to Rosina Storchio, the first Butterfly, on the day it was to be given, 17 February 1904: 'Dear Butterfly, we are forced to kill you on stage, but you, with your profound and exquisite art, will make our opera live.' Tito Ricordi, as producer, had employed a

Puccini with Tito Ricordi.

celebrated Parisian, Lucien Jusseaume, to paint the scenery,
and the other principals were excellent, with Giovanni
Zenatello as Pinkerton, and Giuseppe De Luca as Sharpless.
The conductor was Cleofonte Campanini, who was later to
appear frequently at Covent Garden. Everyone was confident
of success, enthusiasm being such that the orchestra gave
Puccini a standing ovation at the end of the dress rehearsal. He
too sent Storchio a note: 'My wishes are superfluous! Your
great art is so real, delicate and impressive, that the public will
certainly be conquered; and I hope, through you, I am
speeding to victory.'

The fiasco of that first night is one of the most notorious in
operatic history. The initial ominous silence was gradually
interspersed with laughter, hisses and even shouts of derision.

108

When, in Act Two, Storchio's kimono billowed up, there were yells of 'Butterfly is pregnant', and there was little applause for her 'Un bel di'. At the end of her vigil, Tito Ricordi had arranged for imitation birdsong to be heard to greet the dawn, so the audience joined in gleefully with their own bird and animal cries. Ricordi wrote in the March issue of *Musica e Musicisti*:

Growls, shouts, groans, laughter, giggling, the usual single cries of '*bis*', designed to excite the public still more; that sums up the reception which the public of La Scala accorded the new work by Maestro Giacomo Puccini. After this pandemonium, throughout which virtually nothing could be heard, the public left the theatre as pleased as Punch... The spectacle given in the auditorium seemed as well organised as that on the stage, since it began precisely with the beginning of the opera.

He was probably right in attributing this disaster to an organised *claque*. Puccini had become an international figure, who remained aloof from the provincial musical life of Milanese society. Fellow musicians were either jealous of his success, or wanted to see Italian music developing in very different ways to the popular operas he composed. The première represented the moment when Puccini could be brought down from his pedestal and put in his place. The culprit has never been identified, but recently the Italian opera scholar Julian Budden has suggested that the most likely candidate was Ricordi's rival publisher Edoardo Sonzogno. 'Such members of the '*giovane scuola*' as had flocked to his banner – Mascagni, Leoncavallo, Giordano, Cilea – had by now clearly given their best work. None had equalled Ricordi's protégé in achieving three major successes in a row; a fourth was bound to be unwelcome.' Next day, the newspaper headlines proclaimed: 'Puccini hissed', 'Fiasco at La Scala', and 'Butterfly, Diabetic Opera, Result of an Accident'. It all came as a very great shock to Giacomo, and he was never really able to forget the humiliation of that night. He told a friend a few days later that it was 'not so much...what they did to my poor *Butterfly*, but for all the poison they spat on me as an artist and as a man.' While most critics echoed the harsh judgment of the audience, two looked beyond the furore. Commenting that there was little variation between the characters, Nappi in *La perseveranza* stated: 'I am convinced, though, that the public will later appreciate the many beautiful passages, which yesterday were either overlooked or, perhaps, intentionally ignored.' Giovanni Pozza in *Il corriere della sera* found it too

Giuseppe Giacosa with Verdi's last librettist, Arrigo Boito.

Emmy Destinn as Madama Butterfly.

long and drawn out, but concluded: 'I still believe that the opera, once shortened and lightened, will recover – there are too many beautiful pages in it, its structure is too elegant and exquisite... It would be best to wait before pronouncing the final word, better to wait for a calmer and more carefully considered judgment.'

There was no doubt too that the original version, with its long second act, was a mistake. At any rate, it was withdrawn before the second performance, and the next day Puccini was writing to a friend: 'My *Butterfly* remains as it is: the most heartfelt and most expressive opera that I have conceived! I shall win in the end, you'll see – if it is given in a smaller theatre, less permeated by hatred and passion.' After considering Turin and Bologna, Brescia was chosen and Puccini set about revising the score. He reduced Act One by cutting out much relating to the subsidiary characters, Butterfly's friends and relations, which distracted from the flow of the main action. He also omitted many references to the characteristics of the Japanese and Americans, which were offensive to some. Pinkerton, for instance, referred to the 'nauseating gluttony' of the Japanese. The changes to the second act were less. In the original, it was Kate, Pinkerton's wife, who pleaded with the geisha to give up the child. In the revised version, she maintains a dignified and tactful silence, leaving Sharpless to make the request, though no longer humiliating Cio-Cio-San by offering her compensation money. Such changes, though significant, are not enough to account for the different reception the opera subsequently received, nor is the division of the second act into two scenes. Many would argue that Puccini was right in the first place to follow Belasco in giving unity to the whole act, with the vigil marking the transition between the period of waiting and Pinkerton's arrival. Brescia was not too far from Milan, so the critics and many others, including Arrigo Boito, were able to be present for the first night of the second production on 28 May 1902 at the Teatro Grande, with Salomea Krusceniski replacing Rosina Storchio, who was singing in Buenos Aires. 'You seem in your departure to be taking away the best, the most poetical, part of my work', Puccini wrote in a letter to wish her well on her journey. In a theatre a third of the size of La Scala, more suitable for the intimate nature of the opera, it was a triumphant success with several encores of arias, and ten curtain calls for the composer. It was soon being performed all over the world. Rosina Storchio sang in the first foreign production in Buenos Aires, while Covent Garden assembled the superb cast of Emmy Destinn as Butterfly, Caruso as Pinkerton and Scotti as Sharpless.

Self-caricature of Caruso as
Pinkerton.

Advertisement for the first
production of *Madama
Butterfly* at Covent Garden.

A significant change had occurred in Puccini's domestic
arrangements between the completion of *Butterfly* and its
unfortunate première. Elvira's first husband had died in the
previous year, so, on 3 January 1904, in the church at Torre del
Lago, Giacomo and Elvira were married by the parish priest.
Whatever the true state of their relationship at that time, it was
incumbent on the composer to legalise the status of their union
after some 19 years. There is no doubt too that others, his
sister Ramelde in particular, had put pressure on him to marry
Elvira as soon as possible, as one part of the solution to the
affair with Corinna. The ceremony was, perhaps, tinged for
both of them with the same kind of bitter-sweet thoughts that
filled the mind of Giacomo's Japanese heroine, as she waited
for her American lover to return, remembering the original joy,
accepting the present pain, and wondering about the future.

111

Chapter 7

Difficulties with Women

I'm unhappy with *The Girl* in front of me – silent. It's eleven o'clock at night – what great, what immense sadness! Elvira's lawyers are doing their best to ruin her and me by giving conflicting advice... I have done everything I possibly can here by speaking to Doria's brother, but he is implacable. (Puccini in a letter to Sybil Seligman, 16 June 1909.)

Each of the heroines of his previous four operas was, in her own way, an idealisation of the unattainable, inevitably tragic, woman, who represented Puccini's longing for elusive love and fulfilment. Although he was now internationally acclaimed and rich, behind the public image he was filled with self-doubt, often deeply lonely and increasingly preoccupied with fears of his own death. In the years following *Butterfly*, the search for a suitable subject – and heroine – for his next opera was to be more tortuous and wearisome than ever before, while his relationships with women, including Elvira, were to become not only confused, but public.

His world-wide reputation, and a desire to see that his operas – particularly *Butterfly* – should 'suffer the least possible ill-treatment', involved him in extended travels in the period between the première of *Butterfly* and the outbreak of the First World War. An Argentinian newspaper, *La prensa*, lured him to South America for a summer season of his operas in 1905. His fee was stupendous – 50,000 francs, plus the liner fares for him and Elvira, and luxury accommodation in Buenos Aires. Although the voyage was marred by Elvira's seasickness, the month in South America was a tremendous success from the moment they were greeted at the pier by cheering crowds and bands playing Puccini selections. There were productions of five of his operas with Rosina Storchio's triumph as Cio-Cio-San balancing the relative failure of the revised version of *Edgar*. In addition, there were hunting parties to compensate for the endless round of banquets and speeches, which he hated, even though Illica had given him some help in preparing for the latter.

After only a few months back in Torre del Lago, he was off again, this time to London for the second production at Covent Garden of *Madama Butterfly* – he had been in South America at the time of the British première. Both he and his opera were enthusiastically received, and he enjoyed London more on this occasion, writing to Caselli from the Savoy, where he was staying: 'I'm in my real country. How well one lives here, in spite of the fog, which, however, has its own poetry. I have been fêted, wooed and applauded to the point of delirium. Here my soul breathes.' He was interviewed by Wakeling Dry, who published the first English biography of the composer in 1906, describing him as 'a big, broad man, with a frank open countenance, dark kindly eyes of a lazy, lustrous depth, and a shy retiring manner.' Dry was particularly struck with Puccini's modesty, noting that he talked much about the interpreters and performances of his operas, rather than his own compositions, although he did make the revealing remark: 'I am determined not to go beyond the place in art where I find myself at home.'

The Teatro de la Opera, Buenos Aires, 1880.

This London visit was to be especially memorable for the beginning of his long-lasting and close friendship with Sybil Seligman, whose husband David was a wealthy banker. They both spoke fluent Italian, were great Italophiles and welcomed visiting Italian artists to their home. Giacomo first met Sybil at the London house of his friend of many years, Paolo Tosti, now a singing teacher in the English capital, whose pupils included members of the Royal Family and Sybil, a fine contralto and an ardent admirer of Italian opera. Their friendship is partially preserved in the collection of letters from the composer, edited by Sybil's son, Vincent. For a long time, it was thought that their relationship was entirely platonic, but evidence from Sybil's sister to the Puccini scholar Mosco Carner suggested that it began as a passionate love affair. Nevertheless, it was transmuted into a friendship that endured until the composer's death, and was, perhaps, the deepest of his life, certainly with a woman. Unlike Elvira, Sybil was able to understand and help the composer with his professional, as well as his personal, anxieties and concerns. 'The person who has come nearest to understanding my nature' was the compliment he paid her in a letter of 1906, describing her as 'that exquisite and beautiful creature, who is the best friend I have'. Yet Sybil was delicate and sensitive in her dealings with Elvira, always sending her a present when Puccini had visited London, and making sure that the families were friends – they spent holidays together in Nice and Abetone. Nevertheless, there is little doubting the tone of love with which Giacomo wrote to her on his return to Torre in November 1905: 'How I remember everything – the sweetness of your character: the walks in the park, the melodiousness of your voice, and your radiant beauty.'

It was to Sybil, in a letter of January 1906, that he poured out his frustration at being unable to find a suitable libretto: 'I am so utterly depressed by this feverish and disheartening period of searching; not only I, but those who are near me, my publishers and many others, are losing heart.' His search had already covered a bewildering variety of potential subjects. Even before the première of *Butterfly*, he was corresponding with a playwright from Tuscany, Valentino Soldani, about several possible projects, including a proposed *Margherita da Cortona*, set in the twelfth century. Suggestions were not lacking: Ricordi pushed *Romeo and Juliet*, Illica a story by Edgar Allan Poe, while Giacomo himself looked at the old ideas of Giacosa's *La comtesse de Chaillant* and a collaboration with D'Annunzio. None of these suggestions bore fruit. Another subject that he seriously considered for several years

114

was setting three of Maxim Gorky's short stories – Russian literature was very popular in Italy at that time. Although it came to nothing, it was the first time he had thought of a trilogy of one-act operas, a concept that he would later revive. After rejecting the story of William Tell – the subject of Rossini's mammoth French opera of 1829 – and Victor Hugo's tale of the hunchback of Notre-Dame, Puccini proposed to Giacosa, in March 1905, that they might consider a comic opera: 'What do you say to a comic opera? We could try and find a good subject, but one that will make people really laugh. Don't you think this would provide a respite for us as well as the public? By now the graves...and the altars have become filled with dramas of death and languor.' In this context he looked again at *Tartarin*, but Giacosa was seriously ill – he died in September 1906. Puccini did not have enough faith in Illica's ability to pursue this idea any further. Although they did discuss other possible subjects on which to collaborate, they were never to work together again.

Sybil Seligman came up with various ideas – Tennyson's narrative poem *Enoch Arden*, Kipling's novel *The Light that Failed*, Tolstoy's *Anna Karenina* and *The Last Days of Pompeii* by Bulwer-Lytton. Though they were wide-ranging in their literary appeal, and Puccini took them seriously enough, for instance, to read a French translation of the Kipling book, he did not feel that they were suitable. He was much more interested in her subsequent suggestions of *The Duchess of Padua* or *A Florentine Tragedy* by Oscar Wilde, writing to Ricordi from Paris in November 1906: 'I like [*A Florentine Tragedy*] very much. It is in one act, but beautiful, inspired, strong and tragic; three principal characters, three first-rate rôles – it would be a counter-part to *Salome*, yet more human, more real and nearer the feelings of the *man in the street*.' Richard Strauss's opera, based on Oscar Wilde's play, had caused a sensation when first produced in Dresden the previous December. Puccini, whose great-great-grandfather, also Giacomo, had composed a *Salome* in 1741, was to be at the first performance of Strauss's opera at the Metropolitan Opera, New York on 22 January 1907 – after which it was withdrawn as 'a disgrace to civilisation'. *Salome* clearly had a great influence on Puccini, as his next opera would demonstrate. Ricordi was unimpressed with the Oscar Wilde idea, and sent Illica a telegram on 11 December: 'Absolutely necessary for the future good of the Doge [his name for Puccini] to throw Florentine stupidity into fire.' Despite this, Puccini was to return to the idea five years later, but again to no avail.

Of all the numerous proposals explored during these years,

Mary Garden as Salome in the opera by Richard Strauss.

115

the 1898 novel *La Femme et le Pantin* (The Woman and the Puppet) by Pierre Louÿs was the one that engrossed him for the longest time. The story of a Spanish woman, Conchita Perez, and her taunting relationship with a wealthy would-be lover, whom she holds at arm's length until he turns the tables on her, it bears a strong resemblance to *Carmen* – indeed, Conchita, like Bizet's heroine, works in the Seville cigar factory. Discussions with Louÿs in Paris led to the signing of an agreement in June 1906, with the dramatisation to be done by Maurice Vaucaire, who worked on it with the composer at Boscolungo in August. Although Puccini told Ricordi that it was turning out to be very beautiful, he soon began to have doubts, confiding in September to Sybil: 'I am rather preoccupied about *Conchita* [his title] – or, rather, I am feeling weaker on the subject! What frightens me is *her* character, and the plot of the play – and then all the characters seem unlovable, and that is a very bad thing on the stage.' During the following months, he continued to waver, but by 11 April 1907 he had decided to abandon the 'Spanish slut' Conchita, writing Ricordi a long letter setting out his reasons, and concluding that the libretto was too French, 'devoid of any original character', and that they had probably made a mistake in following the novel too closely, 'instead of using our imagination a little more'. The subject was later taken over by a younger composer, Riccardo Zandonai (1883-1944). His wife, Tarquina Tarquini, created the title rôle, after which *Conchita* was given successfully in many countries. Ricordi had hopes that Zandonai, who had studied in Pesaro with Mascagni, would be Puccini's successor in the *verismo* tradition.

Still searching for the next opera subject, Puccini returned, perhaps with a sense of desperation, to Illica's suggestion of Marie Antoinette, deciding this time to concentrate on the ill-fated Queen's final days. He decided to prepare an outline himself, signing an agreement with Illica for the libretto. In May 1907, he sketched the idea to Sybil:

The last days of Marie Antoinette. A soul in torment – first act, prison; second act, the trial; third act, the execution – three short acts, stirring enough to take one's breath away. I'm absolutely taken up with this idea of mine. And I have found a title which seems to me fitting and appropriate because I couldn't call it *Maria Antoinetta*, seeing it deals only with the one episode of her tragic death. The title is *La Donna Austriaca* [The Austrian Woman] – what do you think of it?

This outline is very similar to the plot of Donizetti's opera about the last days of Mary Stuart (*Maria Stuarda*), but it was destined never to see the light of day. In spite of the fact that

116

Illica had been working on it intermittently for almost ten years, Puccini decided that he could not be trusted to produce the libretto without a collaborator, after which nothing more was heard of *La Donna Austriaca*.

The tortuous quest for a libretto was punctuated by further visits to Europe for performances of his operas. These included a trip to Budapest for a week, during which *La bohème*, *Tosca* and *Madama Butterfly* were all given – the composer receiving 40 curtain calls during the latter. In October 1906, he went to Paris for the first French production of *Butterfly* at the Opéra-Comique under the direction of Albert Carré, who fussed about every little detail, until the composer felt it was 'enough to turn one's hair grey'. However, the real problem was his wife, the soprano Marguerite Giraud, who was to sing the title rôle. Although she had excelled as Massenet's Manon, Puccini confided to Sybil that he did not think much of her as an artiste, and duly christened her '*Madame pomme de terre*'. He was depressed at the slow progress made in rehearsals and felt that she wanted 'too many cuts – the reason being she feels that the strain would otherwise be too much for her strength.' His state of mind was not helped by feeling unwell and finding Paris oppressive. His anxiety increased further as his planned short stay in the French capital was perforce extended: 'I'm in a terrible state of panic about Mme Carré; I'm afraid she hasn't the force necessary to go through with the opera.' Sybil sent a patent medicine, which made him feel better, but Mme Carré developed a throat infection, causing a further postponement of the first performance until after Christmas, by which time singer and composer were not on speaking terms. In the event, *Butterfly* was a success with the public, if not with the critics – Rossini and Verdi had been able to compose Italian operas like *Guillaume Tell* and *Les vêpres siciliennes* in a successful French mode, but Puccini, in the eyes of the critics, remained essentially Italian. Carré had not even dared to try *Manon Lescaut* in the French capital, which would have invited a direct comparison with Massenet.

Bored with everything in Paris, Puccini had another pressing reason to leave as soon as possible. Thanks to the initiative of Tito Ricordi and an American impresario, Henry Savage, *Butterfly* had been taken on a seven-month tour of the United States with a total of over 200 performances, something previously unheard-of in the annals of opera. As a grand finale to this tour, though not as part of it, Puccini had been offered 8,000 dollars to supervise a six-week season of *Butterfly* and its three predecessors at the Metropolitan Opera, New York. So, in early January 1907, he and Elvira sailed in the *Kaiserin*

The New York Metropolitan Opera – patrons in the foyer after the opera, waiting for carriages and motors, 1912.

Auguste Victoria in a suite amidships complete with a vomitorium for Elvira, of which, unfortunately, she made much use. Because heavy seas and fog delayed the ship, they arrived in New York only two hours before the first performance of *Manon Lescaut*, slipping into their box in the opera house during the first act, at the end of which the audience stood and applauded the composer for five minutes. 'A magnificent evening,' he wrote to Sybil, 'and a great reception – a really big success – Caruso was amazing, [Lina] Cavalieri good.' *The New York Sun* was full of praise:

What will appeal most forcibly to the musical listener to this work are the crystalline transparency of the scoring, the dainty, delicate, and piquant conceptions of the comedy scenes, the perfect adaptation of means to end in the treatment of the subsidiary voice parts in the concerted bits and ensembles, the virile breadth and force of the love music, and the poignant dramatic expressiveness of the final scene.

Puccini found not being able to speak the language 'beastly', constantly complaining in his letters to Sybil that his nerves were worn to shreds and that he longed for the peace and quiet of Torre. On 18 February, he wrote to her from their hotel, the Astor: 'I've had all I want of America – at the opera all is well, and *Madama Butterfly* was excellent, but lacked the poetry which I put into it. The rehearsals were too hurried, and the woman [Geraldine Farrar] was not what she ought to have been. Also, as regards your *God* [Caruso], (*entre nous*) I make you a present of him – he won't learn anything; he's lazy and he's too pleased with himself – all the same, his voice is magnificent.' This letter is a good example of the way Puccini was often scathingly dismissive of famous singers. Geraldine Farrar had trained under Lilli Lehmann in Berlin and was immensely popular as a member of the Metropolitan Opera from 1906-1922. She was specially adored by young female opera-buffs, who became known collectively as 'Gerry-flappers'. Ironically, Cio-Cio-San was one of the rôles for which she was to be particularly remembered. It was somewhat strange, too, that the composer had so little good to say of Caruso. When the tenor was still a young unknown, he had sung 'Che gelida manina' ('Your tiny hand is frozen' – Rodolfo's aria in Act One of *La bohème*) at Torre del Lago for the composer, who had interrupted him with: 'Who sent you to me? God?' On the strength of this, Caruso secured his first break, as Rodolfo at Leghorn. In spite of Puccini's strictures about the singers in the New York *Butterfly*, the critics were generous in their praise – *The New York Herald* called it 'a sensation', recognising the composer's significant influence on the performance. He had certainly been extremely demanding in rehearsals: Geraldine Farrar recalled in her autobiography that she had been 'utterly worn out by the nervous strain and cruel fatigue of the previous weeks'.

While in New York, Puccini had been shopping with Elvira, and was fascinated by the array of new equipment on display, including the gramophone. For this he predicted a great future, though he pointed out in a letter to *The Herald* the potential problem of royalty collection caused by the mechanical reproduction of music. On one of his trips to New York a wealthy autograph hunter paid him handsomely to write out the first few bars of Musetta's Waltz; money he used to buy a new motor boat, which was shipped to join his already sizeable fleet on Lake Massaciuccoli at Torre. He also went to see three of David Belasco's plays – including *The Girl of the Golden West*, which contained panoramic Californian views on moving curtains, an authentic minstrel band, and a blizzard, requiring 32 stage-hands to operate the wind and snow machines. Belasco claimed that, when a minstrel sang *The Old Dog Tray*

Broadway, New York City, in 1895.

in the first act, Puccini said: 'Ah, there's my theme at last.' That this was another of Belasco's fanciful notions is borne out by a letter from Puccini to Tito Ricordi on 18 February:

Here too I have been trying to find new subjects, but there is nothing useful, or, rather, complete enough. I've found some good hints in Belasco, but nothing definitive, or solid or complete. The atmosphere of the *Wild West* attracts me, but, in all the plays I have seen, I have found only good scenes here and there, never a clear, simple line of development; it's all a muddle, and sometimes in very bad taste and old hat.

On his return to Italy, therefore, he continued to turn over the various possibilities he had already considered, even announcing, on a brief trip to London in June, that he was definitely going to write *La Donna Austriaca*. Belasco's play then began to appear as a strong possibility, as revealed in some doggerel he penned to Sybil (here in a translation by her husband, David):

120

Dearest Syb, I'm far from sorry
To leave at once for rural Torre,
There to bare my manly form,
To the sun, the rain, the storm;
While my Maiden from the West
Lies uneasy on my chest,
And I study *con amore*
France's Revolution's story

It was not until October that Illica and Puccini finally abandoned all hope of completing the Marie Antoinette opera, so for some months the composer was contemplating both stories, though Vincent Seligman recalled that Giacomo could 'talk of nothing but *The Girl*' during the summer holiday the two families spent together at Abetone.

Puccini had requested a copy of the play from Belasco, so that he could study it more carefully in translation. Sybil helped with this, obtaining Red Indian songs, as well as popular songs of the Gold Rush era. In July, Puccini requested his publisher to obtain the rights from Belasco, and contracts were signed the following month. As Illica was still occupied with *La Donna Austriaca*, Tito Ricordi suggested as the librettist Carlo Zangarini, who had the advantage of speaking English, since his mother came from Colorado – he was later to write many libretti, including *Conchita*, Puccini's abandoned subject, for Riccardo Zandonai. Puccini was soon able to

Scene by A.C. Redwood, depicting the Californian Gold Rush, 1890.

121

inform Giulio Ricordi that they were making progress and that 'The Girl promises to be a second Bohème, but more vigorous, more daring, and on an altogether larger scale.' With his eye for effective dramatic moments, he had already decided to combine Belasco's third and fourth acts containing the capture of Dick Johnson, Minnie's successful pleading for his life with the cowboys, and the couple going off together up the path into the mountains. 'I have in mind a magnificent scenario,' he enthused to his publisher, 'a clearing in the great Californian forest, with some colossal trees. But we shall need eight or ten horses on the stage.' His letter also requested Ricordi to gain the author's permission for such changes.

While the librettist was at work, Puccini went to Vienna, where Butterfly was to be given its Austrian première at the Hofoper on 31 October, despite the fact that Mahler, the director, had developed a strong antipathy to Puccini's music after conducting the first German performance of Le villi. He had previously refused to allow any Puccini operas to be given at the Hofoper. Although Puccini found the singers 'hard and unsympathetic', he told Sybil that it was 'a magnificent success', that he had talked with the Queen Mother of Spain, who had told him that 'the Queen is always singing and playing Butterfly', and that he had been given 'a magnificent Ehrbar piano of the Erard type all in yellow olive wood, which goes well in my room at Torre – I'm very pleased with it.' Meanwhile, a note of dissatisfaction began to creep into his relationship with Zangarini, who was, he felt, taking too many liberties with the libretto. Yet by the end of January he had submitted what the composer judged to be 'a really beautiful libretto – it is not fully built, but the foundations have been laid.'

Before he commenced work on 'Minnie and her friends', as he referred to La fanciulla, he and Elvira went to Egypt during February for a fortnight's holiday. After attending a performance of Butterfly in Alexandria, they spent the rest of the time as tourists, which he sketched in a memorable piece of travel writing to his sister, Ramelde:

The pyramids, camels, palms, turbans, sunsets, sarcophagi, mummies, beetles, colossi, columns, tombs of the kings, boats on the Nile, which are nothing but our freddane enlarged, the fez, large gowns men wear, the blacks, the mulattos, the veiled women, the sun, yellow sand, ostriches, the English, the museums, Aida-style arches, Rameses I, II, III, etc., the fertile mud of the Nile, the cataracts, the mosques, the flies, the hotels, the Nile Valley, the ibis, the buffalo, the nagging street vendors, the stench of fat, minarets,

An excursion to the Pyramids with Elvira.

Part of a page from the manuscript of *La fanciulla del West*, illustrating the illegibility of Puccini's hand.

Copt churches, the tree of the Virgin Mary, Cook's ferries, donkeys, sugar cane, cotton, acacias, sycamores, turkish coffee, bands of pipes and drums, religious processions, bazaars, belly dancing, crows, black hawks, ballerinas, Dervishes, Levantines, Bedouins, the Kedive, Ahebes, cigarettes, narghile, hashish, bashish, sphinxes, the immense Fta [the priest's chant in the closing scene of Verdi's *Aida*], Isis, Osiris – they've all broken my balls, and on the 20th I leave to take a rest. Ciao, your Egyptologist.

On their return, he was soon insisting on a second librettist to curb Zangarini's wilder flights of fancy; eventually, a 25-year-old novelist and poet from Livorno, Guelfo Civinini, was appointed, and was soon at work re-casting the first two acts. 'The Girl', Puccini wrote to Elvira from Chiatri, where he had escaped for peace and quiet, 'is more difficult than I thought – it's because of the distinctive and characteristic features, with which I wish to endow the opera that, for the time being, I've lost my way, and don't go straight ahead as I would like.' The heat forced him to Abetone in August but he returned to Torre a month later, where he played Caselli the first act on the piano. During the next month or so, everything seemed to be going well, until his private life caused a major hiatus in the progress of the composition.

Unquestionably, Giacomo had had several extra-marital affaires over the years, but he regarded them as non-threatening to his and Elvira's relationship, as he was to try to explain to her in a letter dated 30 August 1915:

You have never looked at these matters, as do other women who are more reasonable – Good God! The world is full of such things. And all artists cultivate these little gardens, in order to delude themselves into thinking that they are not finished, old and torn by strife. You imagine immense affaires. In reality, it is nothing but a sport, to which all men more or less dedicate a fleeting thought without, however, giving up that which is serious and sacred; that is, the family... Let time and circumstances do their work.

He was constantly having to pacify and reassure her, but gradually his insistence that she was his 'only and true, holy love' gave way to a sadness and despair at her suspicions and accusations. He had written to her from Brussels in 1900:

You write me a letter full of discomfort and sadness. And I? We are two strange beings. But a little of the guilt is yours, dear Elvira. You are no longer the same, your nerves dominate you, no longer a smile, no longer an open mien. In my own house, I feel myself more of a stranger than you do. Oh, the beautiful intimacy of our first years! Now we pass months (at least I do) in a house which belongs to others [her relatives were constantly staying at Torre].

I think always of the beautiful times which are past. In those days we were materially not well off, but, for all that, we were not less content. You are unhappy? I am doubly so... I see no way out. Your letter gave me such pain!

Elvira's jealousy suddenly acquired a new focus. Her demanding nature meant that she found it difficult to keep most servants in her employ. The only exceptions were old Guicche, who turned a deaf ear, and a local girl, Doria Manfredi. She had been with them for five years from the age of 16, when she had been employed, after her father had died, probably because of the extra work involved following Giacomo's accident. She was clearly devoted to them, and was treated much like a daughter of the house. Vincent Seligman remembered that 'there was literally nothing that she would not or could not do, and the whole household revolved round her.' She may well have had a teenage crush on the composer, but, in the autumn of 1908, Elvira, perhaps after insinuations from one of her interfering relatives, suddenly became insanely

jealous of the blossoming girl, convinced that she and her master were having an affaire. After hounding Doria with accusations, Elvira dismissed her. On 6 February 1909, Puccini wrote to Sybil from Rome with an account of what happened next:

Elvira continued to persecute that wretched child, preventing her even from taking a walk, and telling tales about her all over the village – to her mother, her relations, the priest and everyone. All my friends and relations, and I myself, told her to stop it and calm herself; but she wouldn't listen to anyone. I made my peace with her and told her to forget about the past and be satisfied that the girl was no longer in the house. She promised to do so; but the same evening I found her out of doors, hidden in the dark, *dressed in my clothes*, to spy on me. I said nothing, and left the following day for Rome.

Elvira was supposed to go to Milan; instead, she remained for three more days at Torre, and during that time did everything, and said everything she could to the mother, repeating again that her daughter was a * * * * and that we used to meet each other in the evenings in the dark. She told one of Doria's uncles that his daughter used to carry letters between us; and, meeting Doria in the street, she publicly insulted her in the presence of others. Her brother wrote to me in a rage that he would like to kill me, because I was his sister's lover – and that my wife had said so herself. In a word, poor Doria, faced with Hell in her own home and dishonour outside, and with Elvira's insults still ringing in her ears, in a moment of desperation swallowed three tablets of mercuric chloride, and died after five days of atrocious agony.

A post-mortem established that Doria had died a virgin –

125

Elvira's suspicions had been without foundation. The Manfredi family sued her for defamation of character, refusing a large sum offered in settlement by the composer. Elvira fled to Milan with Tonio, who had turned against his father as he thought him guilty, while Puccini stayed at Torre until the trial. Although Doria's brother refused to withdraw the action, and even threatened to kill Elvira if his family lost, he assured Puccini that he wished him well, and that 'before she died, Doria bade him avenge her on her mistress, though no harm must befall her master, because he had always been good to her.' Giacomo tried to persuade Elvira to admit her mistake and claim that she had been deceived into mistreating Doria, but it was to no avail. She even made the mistake of not attending the trial on the grounds of ill health. She was found guilty, sentenced to five months and five days imprisonment, and ordered to pay 700 lire in damages, plus costs. Incredibly, her obsession and delusion still continued, for she wrote to her husband two days later:

This last blow has demolished me, and surely I shall not get over it easily. Everybody has condemned me...and now what shall we do? Appeal? What will be my defence? Tell the truth? But you know this, now more than ever, is impossible without hurting chiefly you. What will the world say? That you let your wife be condemned? And shall I have to go to prison? That you do not desire, I hope.

Her lawyers advised her to admit the libel, but to appeal against the counts of defamation of character and threat to life and limb, but, having won exoneration for their daughter, the Manfredi family finally decided to accept Puccini's substantially increased offer of 12,000 lire, and withdrew the action in October 1909.

Since Puccini was such an essentially private and shy person, the widespread publicity about this scandal, not only in Italy but all over the world, was immensely painful to him. People who saw him remarked that he had suddenly aged. His own verdict was: 'I have been through the most tragic days of my life. I'm better now, but my gorge rises at the thought of all the barbarities committed.' A reconciliation with Elvira was achieved after several failed attempts, though it was not until the last years of his life that some of the affection returned to their marriage. At the end of July 1909, Puccini reported to Sybil, in a letter from Bagni di Lucca: 'Now all three of us are reunited again here, and it seems as if life is going to be less unpleasant. Elvira seems to me to have changed a great deal as a result of the hardships of the separation which she has

126

Elvira with Giacomo and their son Antonio at Torre del Lago.

endured – and so I hope to have a little peace and to be able to get on with my work.' The effect on his composition had been no less devastating. While the 'Affair Doria' lasted, from October 1908 to July 1909, his letters had been full of complaints that *The Girl* had 'completely dried up', that he was only able to work a little, and that he wondered if it would ever be finished. But things greatly improved in the summer, so that, on 30 September, he was able to tell Sybil that he had nearly finished the second act 'where there's a love duet, which seems to me to have come out well'.

He took time off in October to go to Brussels for the first Belgian performance of *Madama Butterfly*, writing Sybil a most significant letter. After saying that he hoped the opera would be 'a real triumph', because he had worked hard with the cast and made the theatre change all the scenery, which he found ugly, he continued: 'I am getting on all right with Elvira... Life is fairly boring, but at least we don't have squabbles and rows – of which I've had more than my fair share! I'm working constantly, and I'm longing to be back at Torre so as to return to my Minnie. I've nearly got to the third act – a good step forward, in fact.' Then he makes the only surviving reference to Elvira being jealous about their relationship. 'I'm sorry that

Lucrezia Bori as Manon.

Elvira has taken our friendship amiss. But this fancy of hers too will, I hope, disappear one day – and if it doesn't, it's enough for us to remain what we have always been – affectionate friends, full of good and sincere feelings towards each other, and whenever we meet it will be a treat for us – that's right, isn't it?' In the knowledge that their friendship had originally been a passionate one, this letter seems to indicate that they had recognised the necessity to ensure it now remained platonic.

Back at Torre he found the work of composition tortuous, but, at least, he wrote to Sybil, 'I have my Minnie – the rest is emptiness.' Though he told her that he was living like a hermit 'without emotions and without anything else', by April he still had not begun the third act, though he had done some orchestration. A break was provided by a trip to Paris in June for a season of Italian opera at the Théâtre du Châtelet by the Metropolitan Opera Company, the highlight of which proved to be *Manon Lescaut* with Caruso as Des Grieux and a 22-year-old, Lucrezia Bori, as Manon. Puccini found her 'exquisite', though her dress was far too grand for the down and out, dying Manon of the final act. He tried to rectify this by throwing a cup of coffee over it to make it look more realistic. He commented to Sybil: 'Last night was an enormous success – the receipts were 65,000 francs. Those pigs – the gentlemen of the Press – were full of bile against me, and who cares a fig, if the public takes my side in this way?'

By August 1910, he had finished the opera, but the choice of a title proved to be a problem. Belasco's *The Girl of the Golden West* did not sound so well in Italian as in English – *La fanciulla dell'occidente d'oro* – while *La fanciulla dell'occidente* did not communicate the Wild West. It was Sybil Seligman who suggested the excellent compromise of a hybrid title, and so it became *La fanciulla del West*. Puccini dedicated it to the wife of King Edward VII of England, Queen Alexandra, a lover of opera, who had declared herself to be particularly fond of *La bohème*. In June 1911, he was to inform Sybil: 'I've had an autograph letter from Queen Alexandra – most flattering indeed to me. It was nice – really awfully nice; I was genuinely touched by it. There was also an elegant diamond and ruby pin.' The première was to be given in New York with Caruso and Emmy Destinn, the renowned Czech soprano who was not only a fine singer but also an accomplished actress. The conductor was to be Arturo Toscanini, who visited Torre del Lago to study the score with the composer before leaving for America.

Puccini, his son Tonio, and Tito Ricordi sailed on the

George Washington in November. Elvira was left behind, a fact she clearly resented, telling her husband in a letter of 30 November she was 'bored and always alone'. 'The only thing that consoles me is the thought that at least you are happy without me – I wish everything goes well, just as you desire, that you enjoy a great triumph, and that no shadow, even the faintest, comes to disturb your peace. Now you are a great man, and, compared to you, I am nothing but a pygmy. Therefore be happy and forgive me if I have annoyed you with my lamentations.' For his part, Giacomo was clearly much taken with the luxury of the ocean voyage in the Imperial Suite, which he described in a letter to Giulio Ricordi:

A princely bath, a room with two gilt bedsteads with various sorts of opaline-tinted lamps; drawing-room with luxurious divans and mikado mirrors; dining-room with furniture in the best English taste, ingenious cupboards which are even lighted inside, everything comfortable, large, and spacious as in the most modern of hotels. Price, £320 for passage alone. Large windows with sumptuous silk curtains. In short, a stupendous suite! Praise to the Metropolitan!

At the world première of *La fanciulla del West* – Puccini, Toscanini, Belasco and the manager of the Met, Gatti-Casazza, previously manager of La Scala.

William Frederick Cody (Buffalo Bill), American Scout and showman, whose show had introduced Puccini to the Wild West in 1889.

If Puccini never really came to terms with worldly success and appeared at times to be struck dumb by public acclaim, Tito Ricordi took a very different attitude. They were given an extravagant welcome tea party by the wealthy Directors of the Metropolitan, but Tito grabbed the horrified composer by the arm and led him out, saying that they had come to rehearse and work, not to waste time on official receptions. He later confessed that he had wanted once in his life to 'smack a million dollars in the face!' The rehearsals went well and, before long, David Belasco had become involved in the production, working on improving the singers' acting technique, demonstrating, for example, to Pasquale Amato, as Sheriff Jack Rance, how to slap Dick Johnson, played by Caruso. He also insisted that one of the cowboys put the noose over Johnson's neck in the final scene, since it would have caused great offence for this to be done by the Red Indian, Billy Jack Rabbit, as Puccini had directed. Similarly, the miners' costumes were changed during rehearsals, because Puccini had not understood that gold-miners would not wear the cowboy rig-out of cattle ranchers – to him the Wild West was all one.

The première on 10 December 1910 was a glittering occasion and, in spite of elaborate precautions, tickets were re-sold for large sums. There were 52 curtain calls in all, during which the manager, Gatti-Casazza, placed a silver wreath with ribbons in the national colours of the USA and Italy on Puccini's head. The newspaper headlines the next day spoke of 'Great Welcome for New Opera', 'America Proud of *The Girl of the Golden West*' and 'Riots over Puccini', but the fulsome praise of some critics was tempered by the reservations of others. Puccini had made it clear that he had tried to write an opera that reflected the spirit of the American people, but that the music, with the exception of one or two themes, remained essentially Italian. Yet *The Musical Courier* felt that American operas should be written by Americans, and expressed the opinion that Puccini's opera 'caters to a depraved taste, and the music is without any appeal beyond that of emphasizing the meretricious elements in the libretto.' It has remained a matter of debate whether Puccini took a step forward in *La fanciulla*, by ensuring that it was always the music that advances and comments on the action, rather than the emotions of the characters, or whether his devices for doing this remain clever but not profound. Richard Aldrich in *The New York Times* pointed to the development of the composer's musical style:

130

In *Madama Butterfly*, it was observed that he had ventured far into a region of new and adventurous harmonies. He has now gone still further into this field of augmented intervals and chords of higher dissonances. He has made use of the so-called 'whole tone' scale and the harmonies that associate themselves with it. In a word, there is a marked predilection for the idiom that is coupled with the name of Debussy.

La fanciulla del West was given immediately in several other American cities. Its first European performances were at Covent Garden on 29 May 1911, for which the composer was present, and at the Teatro Costanzi in Rome a fortnight later with Toscanini conducting. It went all round the world in the next few years, though, unlike its predecessors, it failed to become part of the established repertoire of opera houses, until a recent spate of productions has remedied that neglect.

The steamship *Lusitania*, on which Puccini returned to Europe.

Puccini returned to Europe on the *Lusitania*, writing a glowing letter to Toscanini's wife, Carla, full of appreciation for her husband, but disclosing, once again, that inner emptiness with which he always had to wrestle, particularly after times of great public adulation: 'I envy you, for I would like to be like you, with your closely knit family, with your children who love you so, and with your friends who believe in you. I, alas, feel alone in this world, and that is why I am always sad.' It is notable both that *La fanciulla del West* is the only Puccini opera in which a death does not occur, and that, whereas there is a wealth of incident throughout the opera, the emotions of individuals are uncharacteristically less developed than in his other mature operas. Perhaps the pain of the composer's own life at this period subconsciously restrained him from probing the deeper and darker side of 'Minnie and her friends'.

Chapter 8

No Fluttering of the Spirit

I judge from the feeling which weighs upon my spirit as I work, that our labours are not prospering. I am not happy. I am not laughing. I am not interested. We need something better than this, dear Beppino, in our weary world! (Puccini in a letter to Giuseppe Adami about *La rondine*, 25 September 1914.)

'At the point at which I have now arrived in art, I need to find something loftier, more musical, and more original,' Puccini wrote to Sybil Seligman on 8 February 1911, apologising that, in spite of the fact that she had taken the trouble to make an Italian translation of Sudermann's *Johannisfeuer* (The Fires of St John), it did not have an interesting enough plot to put to music. 'If only you knew how pleased I would be to be able to say: "*It's all right*" and it's what I'm looking for', but 'there is no fluttering of the spirit behind the words, that something which evokes music, the divine art which begins, or ought to begin, where the words cease.' As soon as he had finished *La fanciulla*, he had renewed the tedious search for the next suitable libretto – so difficult to find since *Butterfly*. Sybil also suggested the West Country novel *Lorna Doone* by Richard Blackmore, and a tale from the *Arabian Nights*, but to no avail. Puccini became quite enthusiastic about *Liliom*, a play by the Hungarian Ferencz Molnár, but the author refused to allow the possibility of a play of his being remembered only as an opera by Puccini.

He had been interested in the idea of a comic opera for some time, and had told a New York reporter that he was tired of tragic subjects and wanted a 'good, lusty comedy'. By November 1911, he was asking Sybil if she knew of 'any grotesque novel or story or play, full of humour and buffoonery? I have a desire to laugh and to make other people laugh.' What attracted him eventually was a comedy by the Spanish playwrights Joaquin and Serafin Quintero – *Anima*

Cartoon of Puccini by Sen.

allegra (The Cheerful Soul). Giulio Ricordi recommended as librettist a 33-year-old playwright and music critic, Giuseppe Adami (1878-1946), who had helped him with the libretto of one of his own unfinished operas. Adami was to become a devoted friend of Puccini, and was to publish the first collection of his letters, the *Epistolario*, in 1928, as well as one of the early biographies. To begin with, the composer wanted him to collaborate with Zangarini, but, in the event, it was Adami alone who devoted a year's work to *Anima allegra*. Yet Puccini rejected it, because the tale of Spanish gypsies was reminiscent of *Carmen*, even though the plots were not at all similar and Adami offered to reset it in Holland. In 1921, Adami's libretto was set to music by the Director of the Istituto Musicale in Pavia, Franco Vittadini, and became his greatest operatic success. Its moments of Puccinian tenderness leave the uneasy feeling that Puccini may have made a mistake in turning down this Spanish story.

Another reason for the abandonment of *Anima allegra* may well have been that Giulio Ricordi, who had been a promoting it as a subject, died on 12 June 1912. He had discovered, supported and encouraged Puccini, drawing on his great wisdom and insight into opera, as well as his enormous professional knowledge and skill. It was small wonder that Giacomo had often referred to him as 'Papà Giulio': their correspondence demonstrates mutual affection and esteem, so that their friendship survived even the major disagreement over Corinna, as well as Ricordi's pungent criticism of the last act of *Tosca*. Two months earlier, Giacomo had also lost one of the other people closest to him, his favourite sister, Ramelde. His other sisters were conventional and remote, but he had been able to confide in Ramelde, even though she had not been afraid to play an active part in separating him from Corinna.

If these two deaths left gaps that could not be filled, he had found some solace elsewhere. During the summer of 1911, he had met a German baroness, Josephine von Stängel, on the beach at the nearby seaside resort of Viareggio. She came from Munich, was 35 years old to Puccini's 52, had two small daughters, but was separated from her husband. Their affaire was of necessity clandestine and intermittent. Nevertheless, it was serious enough that, in 1915, Josephine took steps towards obtaining a divorce and they began to talk of a home together in Viareggio. Three surviving letters from her reveal a passionate relationship with 'Giacomucci' or 'Mucci', as she called him. 'I adore your art, your music, your great knowledge, and above all I love...your modesty and your simplicity in everything you do... And your love for me is the most sacred of

Arnold Schoenberg
(1874-51)

poems, and your goodness is so sweet that it makes me your slave.' Their affaire continued for several years, until the First World War made it increasingly difficult, so that it was with Elvira that Giacomo was to end his days at Viareggio. Yet he was not even 'faithful' to 'Josi', since he was writing secretly at the same time to Blanka Lendvai, a Hungarian, whose brother had been most supportive during the Doria scandal. While Josephine was writing to him saying, 'I would like to have your dear mouth and your tender eyes now', Puccini was capable of writing to Blanka, 'I kiss your beautiful mouth'.

His fear of growing old and the consequent loss of his physical and mental powers may well have been eased by such relationships, but his search for 'more original' subjects was in part dictated by his dread that he might have lost his creative instinct. In the first decades of the twentieth century, the musical climate was changing radically. Although it was not produced until 1924, Arnold Schoenberg's opera *Erwartung* (Expectation), written in 1909, abandoned tonality in its exploration of the nightmare world of a woman's mind on the

Portrait of Stravinsky by Picasso, circa 1925.

135

borderlines of sanity. At this time too, Igor Stravinsky's three great early ballets, *The Firebird*, *Petrushka* and *The Rite of Spring* had roused much controversy and challenged past convention. Stravinsky completed the first act of his opera *The Nightingale* in Russia in 1909, but did not compose the final two acts until he was in Switzerland in 1914. Act One had been written while the influence of his teacher Rimsky-Korsakov, who had died the previous year, was still recognisable. The stylistic leap to the next two acts demonstrates graphically the gulf that was opening up between young, modern composers and those, like Puccini, whose roots lay firmly in the tradition of the latter part of the nineteenth century.

Puccini's fear that his operas might be thought old-fashioned was a very real one, and was reinforced by the publication in 1912 of a scathing attack on his music by Fausto Torrefranca, an *avant-garde* Italian music critic, then aged 29. In the preface to his book, *Giacomo Puccini e l'opera internazionale*, he stated that Puccini seemed to embody 'all the decadence of modern Italian music and represents all its barefaced commercialism, all its miserable impotence and the triumph of internationalism.' Torrefranca took as his starting point the assertion that the true spirit of Italian music was to be found in the tradition of instrumental works begun in the seventeenth and eighteenth centuries by composers like Frescobaldi, Corelli and Vivaldi. He was articulating the feelings of the next generation of composers – Casella, Malipiero and Pizzetti – who felt that opera had dominated Italian music for too long, and that it had been unduly influenced by late German Romanticism and French Impressionism. Consequently, they maintained, it was not really 'Italian'. Torrefranca, therefore, inveighed against Puccini's 'facile universalism', as he perceived it, 'which requires of the spectators only the minimum of attention necessary to pass the time agreeably.' That international critics had accused him of remaining too Italian was of small comfort to the composer at the time, and he was not to know that the very people ranged against him were to fail to deliver the *risorgimento* (renaissance) of Italian music, for which they called. He was stunned and hurt by this outright attack, which received worldwide attention, and, though he expressed his anger to friends, in public he maintained a dignified silence.

Numerous subjects for the next libretto were considered and rejected, including *Rip Van Winkle*, *Les Trois Mousquetaires* and a scenario set in Russia by Illica and a critic, Giovanni Pozza, which Puccini dismissed as having 'no power to strike with tremendous force'. In a letter dated 8 October 1912, he set out for his former librettist the guiding principles he was pursuing in his hunt for his next opera subject:

I assure you that our musty old *mises en scène* have become tiresome, and for me there is something to praise and to derive profit from, if one tries to abandon the old ways (so long as this is done with critical taste and not out of a thirst for the new at all costs). Don't you know about the things they have done and are doing in Russia and in London and in Germany? I admire any kind of attempt toward unhackneyed *productions*.

To turn to ourselves: I told you that I still want to *make people weep*: therein lies everything. But do you think that this is easy? It's terribly difficult, dear Illica. In the first place, where is one to look for a subject? And will our imagination find that sacrosanct, that enduring thing? We are not out to make original departures, nor do we rack our brains searching for something new. Love and grief were born with the world, and we, our kind who have passed the half-century, know well the impact of both the one and the other. We must, therefore, find a story which holds us with its poetry and its love and grief, and inspires us to the point that we might make an opera of it. But I repeat to you (not that I have any doubt in you, never!), I feel a little shaken in my faith and it begins to desert me! Do you think that during all this time (since the last note of *Fanciulla*) I have sat with my hands crossed in my lap? I have tried all and everything, and what has so far remained on my fingers is nothing but the ashes of the dead. Addio, I feel weary and in despair.

This was, in reality, the end of their collaboration, and, whereas Puccini was eventually able to move on to a fresh stage in his creative life, Illica, who had written four Puccini libretti and some 75 others, had passed his heyday and was ignored by the new generation of modern composers.

Puccini felt able to pursue the idea of a trilogy of operas after the death of Giulio Ricordi, who had thought it not a commercially viable project owing to the probable length of performance. During the autumn of 1912, the composer saw the one-act play *La houppelande* (The Cloak) by Didier Gold at the Théâtre Marigny in Paris, where it was enjoying a long run. It was the melodramatic story of the murder of a wife and her lover by her jealous husband on a Seine barge. The atmosphere and local colour appealed to Puccini, as it had to Parisian audiences – he described it to Illica as 'almost, no, more than almost, *Grand Guignol*'. It is said that Didier Gold walked him along the banks of the Seine to give him the feel of the setting. By June of the next year he had consulted D'Annunzio about a second libretto, and the French playwright Tristan Bernard, about a comic one. Though nothing came of these proposals,

Guilio Ricordi

he continued to look for subjects for two other short operas. A little progress was made with *Il tabarro* (the Italian title of *La houppelande*), though there was a false start with a writer and politician, Ferdinando Martini, who had put himself forward as a librettist. After a year had produced almost nothing in the way of results, he acknowledged that the writing of libretti was not his *forte*, and yielded to Giuseppe Adami. Despite this change of librettist, it was to be some time before the opera saw the light of day.

Meanwhile, Puccini was researching another possibility that seemed a fairly odd choice – *Two Little Wooden Shoes* (*Due zoccoletti* in Italian) by the popular English romantic novelist Louise de la Ramée, known better under her pseudonym Ouida. It tells of a flower-girl from Brabant, betrayed by a French painter, who commits suicide after wearing out her

The novelist Ouida, in her more affluent days.

clogs by walking to Paris and back to find him. Ouida had decided that life in England was too artificial, so she frittered away her royalties first in Florence, then in Lucca, and finally in Massarosa on the opposite side of Lake Massaciuccoli to Torre del Lago. In 1908, she died destitute at Viareggio. In March 1914, Puccini wrote to Sybil Seligman, asking her to enquire about the exclusive rights to Ouida's novel from her publisher, 'a Mr Macmillan who lives in St Martin's Street'. She found out that it was, in fact, Chatto & Windus who had published *Two Little Wooden Shoes*, but it later became evident that the copyright rested with a lawyer in Viareggio, to whom Puccini gave 1,000 lire to try to establish his claim – unsuccessfully as it turned out – over those of the other interested parties.

There were two probable reasons why Puccini was keen to get the exclusive copyright of the novel himself. In the first place, an American film company had offered him one million lire (£40,000), a staggering sum in those days, to write the music to accompany a silent film, so he may well have thought that an opera based on Ouida's story could also be made into a money-making film. Her novel *Under Two Flags* – about the Spanish legion – *was* turned into a Hollywood film, and would have made her fortune had she lived. Secondly, Puccini was keen that Tito Ricordi should not gain control of the rights. Their relationship had been worsening, partly because Tito was promoting Riccardo Zandonai as his protégé, and partly because his ruthless, business-like approach was unsympathetic to Puccini's continual vacillation over the choice of a subject. After the completion of *La fanciulla del West*, Tito had wanted an immediate contract for the next opera, whereas Puccini and Giulio had never signed an agreement until both were fairly sure that an opera would ensue. When Puccini announced in *Il corriere della sera* in March 1914 that he was planning this opera, Mascagni immediately announced that he had found the subject first. 'Let him go ahead if he wants to,' Giacomo wrote to Sybil. 'I have nothing to be afraid of – by now I have become accustomed to doubles: two *Manon*s, two *Bohème*s, the...four *little wooden shoes*.'

The Viennese publishing firm Herzmansky-Doblinger made him an offer of 400,000 crowns (£16,000) plus 40 per cent royalties for the contract on this work. Giacomo wrote to Sybil that 'it will be a nice little sum of money to put by for a rainy day.' Although he felt that Tito Ricordi had brought the loss of the rights on his own head, he eventually turned the German offer down and would have signed an agreement with Tito for half the amount, 'because of a certain peculiar sentimentality of mine', as he put it to Sybil. In view of the conflicting claims of Puccini, Mascagni, Ricordi and the Leipzig publisher of Ouida's works on the Continent, a court in Viareggio decided that an auction of the copyright should be held for the benefit of Ouida's Italian creditors. The Ricordi representative made the successful bid of 4,000 lire, only to hand over the document with an extravagant gesture to Puccini. Typically, by the end of the year, he had lost interest in the subject, and it was Mascagni, after all, who wrote *Lodoletta* (The Little Lark) based on *Two Little Wooden Shoes*. His librettist was Giovacchino Forzano, the literary expert called in by the judge in Viareggio to advise him over the copyright. He later reappeared as the librettist for two of the operas in Puccini's *Il trittico*.

The first production of *La fanciulla del West* at the Hofoper had interrupted work on *Il tabarro*, by taking Puccini to Vienna in October 1913, where, no doubt, he had taken the opportunity to meet Josephine. The Minnie was Maria Jeritza, the young Czech soprano noted not only for her lovely voice and physical beauty, but also for her considerable acting ability. She had created the title rôle in *Ariadne auf Naxos* by Richard Strauss at Stuttgart in 1912, and would also be the first Empress in his *Die Frau ohne Schatten* (The Woman without a Shadow) in Vienna in 1919. She reached the height of her fame in the inter-war years, not only as the first American Jenůfa, Marietta and Turandot, but also for rôles as varied as Tosca, Thaïs, Carmen and Fedora. In her biography, *Sunlight and Song*, she recalled that Puccini worked tirelessly with her on the rôle of Minnie: 'He went over the music step by step, phrase by phrase. He moulded me. I was his *creation*. Sometimes, he would make me so angry I wanted to cry; then he would get angry. "Jeritza," he would say, "if ever I wake you

Maria Jeritza, the Czech soprano.

at three in the morning and ask you to sing a high C, you *will* sing a high C."' It was she who, having tripped and fallen during a rehearsal of *Tosca* the following spring, sang 'Vissi d'arte' from a prone position, which Puccini liked and asked her to keep in the performance, a practice followed subsequently by many Toscas. Puccini was later to proclaim her as his best Tosca and 'one of the most original artists I have ever known'.

While he was in Vienna, he was offered a large cash payment and 50 per cent royalties for an operetta, for which he would have to write only eight or ten musical numbers. The approach came from the directors of the Carltheater, Otto Eibenschütz and Heinrich Berté – the latter was to win worldwide fame for his *Lilac Time* (*Das Dreimäderlhaus*), about Schubert's life.

140

Puccini turned down their proposal, but his Viennese friend, Baron Eisner von Eisenhof, continued to act as intermediary, until Puccini returned the following spring for *Tosca*.

Tito Ricordi, who had not accompanied him as he was supervising a production of *Francesca da Rimini* by Zandonai in Naples, had sent Carlo Clausetti in his place, as the Ricordi representative. Two days before the *Tosca* performance, Tito summoned Clausetti by telegram. Puccini wired back, asking Tito to allow him to stay for two more days, until after the first performance. Tito replied with another telegram: 'Impossible to accede to request. I order Clausetti to leave immediately.' Probably to take his revenge on Tito, Puccini then signed an agreement with the Carltheater directors for a subject of their choice, *La rondine* (The Swallow), to be dramatised by their librettists (Alfred Willner and Heinz Reichert, the future librettists of *Lilac Time*). The Italian version was to be by a dramatist of Puccini's choosing – Giuseppe Adami – 'who must be permitted a reasonably free hand in his adaptation'. Giacomo wrote to Sybil that he would offer the option to Tito on the 'fantastic terms' of the Viennese, but he conjectured that the publisher certainly would not agree, and then he would 'be free and feel no scruples – indeed, the debt of gratitude I owe to the house of Ricordi has been more than fully paid through the large and continuous revenue they derive from my old operas – don't you agree? And now Tito is most inconsiderate in his treatment of me – he behaves as though I were nothing but a bit of scrap iron.'

The plot of *La rondine* bears a strong resemblance to Verdi's *La traviata*. Magda, the swallow of the title, flies from her feathered nest as the mistress of a Parisian banker, to find true love in the country with a poor young poet, Ruggero, only to return to her wealthy lover when the poet's mother gives permission for her to marry Ruggero, as long as she is 'good, meek, pure and has all the virtues'. Interwoven is a sub-plot about the maid, Lisette, which owes an obvious debt to the plot of Johann Strauss's operetta *Die Fledermaus*. At first Puccini was positive about *La rondine*, writing to Sybil from Milan in September 1914: 'It's a light, sentimental opera with touches of comedy – but it's agreeable, limpid, easy to sing, with a little waltz music, and lively, fetching tunes. We'll see how it goes.' Doubts soon began to creep in, and Puccini's letters, from November onwards, are full of comments about how difficult he was finding it and how discouraged he was. He had realised that the drama was very 'thin', with a fatal flaw at the end where no convincing motive was established for Magda to desert Ruggero. He considered sending the contract

141

back to Vienna so that he would be free to start thinking of something else. He wrote to Adami on 19 November: '*La rondine* is a piece of obscene trash (*porcheria*). I curse the day when I signed the contract with the Viennese.' The librettist rose to the occasion, and, abandoning the proposed operetta with spoken dialogue, re-fashioned it as a light opera set to music throughout, 'like *Rosenkavalier* but more amusing and organic', as Puccini described it. Delighted to have more for their money, the Viennese readily agreed to alter the contract. Adami was recognised as the sole librettist, while Reichert and Willner would be responsible for the German version. Puccini still demanded that countless passages be re-written; so that Adami, in retrospect, judged that nothing had been 'more exhausting, more worrying, more arduous, more infuriating, more difficult and more desolating' than helping this little bird take wing.

Puccini's difficulties with *La rondine* were not limited to its composition. At the beginning of the First World War, Italy was neutral with its population divided between those who favoured the Allies and those who supported Germany and Austria. Unlike Verdi, Puccini did not possess a deep-seated nationalistic fervour, and, before the outbreak of War, international events seemed largely to pass him by, while he remained preoccupied with his music and his circle of friends. Yet, after the commencement of hostilities, although he still had personal concerns – his desire for the War to end so that he could resume his foreign travels, meet friends like Sybil again, and see his operas produced in all countries – there was also a thread of genuine compassion at the sufferings of humanity. He wrote to Sybil in December 1914: 'War is too horrible a thing, whatever the results; for, whether it be victory or defeat, human lives are sacrificed. We live in a terrible world, and I see no sign of this cruel state of things coming to an end!' Nevertheless, there were several critical points when his attitude *was* called into serious question.

The first involved Toscanini, who was staying in Viareggio during the summer of 1914. They discussed the chaos in Italy at length, but, when Puccini – who had always been very popular in Germany and Austria – said he hoped the Germans would soon come and sort it out, the anti-German conductor was outraged. It was some years before they were friends again. The second episode was much more public. At the end of 1914, Hall Caine, an English novelist, conceived the idea of *King Albert's Book*, to which the famous of the world would contribute, as an expression of support for the Belgian King and his people. Composers like Debussy, Elgar, Mascagni and

Saint-Saëns did so, but Puccini declined, saying he wished, as an Italian, to remain neutral. He was attacked in the French Press as a supporter of the Central Powers. As he tried to explain to Sybil in a letter of 11 February 1915, he was something of an internationalist: 'I have feelings of friendship and gratefulness for the reception given to my music everywhere – in France, in England, in Austria and in Germany.'

Once Italy joined the War on the side of the Allies, his neutral position was less tenable, but he still resisted Tito Ricordi's suggestion that he make an anti-German statement, as Leoncavallo had done. Italy's entry into the First World War did mean that the Viennese had to resign their rights to the première. Puccini had retained the Italian and South American rights, so he offered these to Tito Ricordi, who refused them, telling him that his opera had not come off, and it was 'bad Lehár'. Consequently, Puccini signed a contract with the publishing house of Lorenzo Sonzogno, which was a separate branch of the Sonzogno firm, the sponsors of the competition for one-act operas, in which Puccini's *Le villi* had failed to gain even an honourable mention in 1883. It had been created to promote Italian and foreign operettas in particular. After the first production of *La rondine* in 1917, Léon Daudet, son of Alphonse, author of *Tartarin de Tarascon*, made a violent protest in a series of articles in *L'Action Française* about this presentation of an Austrian-commissioned work. Puccini sent a strong letter to several French newspapers pointing out that,

The tenor Tito Schipa, who created the rôle of Ruggero in *La rondine*.

although the Viennese had originally commissioned an operetta with a libretto written by Austrians, it had been changed into an opera with an Italian librettist. He concluded: 'The accusation of M. Daudet boils down to this: I have taken away from our enemies that which was their property, and given my opera to an Italian publisher. If that is my crime, I have reason to be proud of it.' He did, however, make several conciliatory gestures, giving to wounded soldiers a year's royalties from performances of *Tosca* at the Paris Opéra-Comique, donating to bereaved families the proceeds from the 25th anniversary performance of *Manon Lescaut* in Turin, and composing for the benefit of the Italian Red Cross a contribution for a collection of songs published by Ricordi.

In Holy Week 1916, Puccini had been able to tell Sybil that *La rondine* was finished, and was only 'waiting for the end of the War to undertake its first flight, either into the heavens or down to earth.' Lorenzo Sonzogno liaised with the Viennese in neutral Switzerland and arranged for the première to be given at Monte Carlo on 27 March 1917, with Gilda Dalla Rizza as Magda, Ina Maria Ferraris as Lisette, Tito Schipa as Ruggero and the Sicilian conductor Gino Marinuzzi. Because of the War, there were few foreign critics present, but Claude Trevor from *The Musical Standard* stated that 'it will not be long before the suave melodies of Puccini's last success will be heard everywhere where flowing, melodious music still appeals'; while *L'Éclaireur de Nice* stated that 'the swallow seems to have taken wing on its flight across the world.' Although it was given in several countries, achieving most success in Buenos Aires, the first Italian production at Bologna in June 1917 was a disappointment, and the series of performances in Milan in October at the Teatro dal Verme, with a cast that included Beniamino Gigli as Ruggero and Toti dal Monte as Lisette, was a disaster. It was performed in a German version (as *Die Schwalbe*) at the Volksoper in Vienna after the War without much success. It did not reach New York until 1928, and has never been performed at Covent Garden. Though Puccini tried to improve it by making several alterations over the years, *La rondine* has not gained a place in the international repertoire. His little bird may have made a few tentative flights, but, in his own words, there was in it 'no fluttering of the spirit' to allow it to take wing in soaring flight like its predecessors.

Chapter 9

Old Things in a New Way

Without fever there is no creation, because emotional art is a kind of malady, an exceptional state of mind, an over-excitation of every fibre and every atom of one's being. (Puccini in a letter to Giuseppe Adami dated 10 November 1920.)

Since the War curtailed his foreign travel, as well as many productions of his operas, Puccini spent more time at home. He wrote to Sybil in April 1916:

How I long to travel! When will this cursed War be over? It seems to me like a suspension of life!... When shall we be able to travel about again without hindrance as we used to do? How one longs again for a little life! Here one languishes; between the green earth and the sea, the seeds of hatred against this enforced calm are beginning to develop within me.

The old Torre del Lago, with Puccini's villa in the centre background.

This did, of course, mean that he was able to spend more time on those outdoor pursuits he loved. In the autumn of 1915, he went to the Maremma – 'a wild and primitive country, far, far away from the world; where the spirit really finds rest and the body strength.' He had 'a great time' there, shooting snipe, and roaming through the woods. Another consequence of this enforced confinement at home appears to have been the decision to begin work on his one-act operas, while he was still composing *La rondine*. If the idea of three short, contrasting operas based on the stories of Maxim Gorky had come to nothing ten years previously, the idea of an operatic trilogy remained with him. He had begun *Il tabarro* in the autumn of 1913, but was diverted by the abortive Ouida project and *La rondine*, so it was not until the second half of 1915 that he took it up again. It is evident that he did not find the libretto powerful enough, for he urged Adami to make it 'more passionate, inspired and lively' at various points: 'I beseech you, therefore, *with feet and hands clasped*, to put some warmth into them and give me a winged end, or if you can't find wings, at least make it effective.' By May 1916, he had finished the first half, reporting to his collaborator that it had turned out well, and he was more than satisfied with it. He finished it on 25 November that year, though after the first performance he was to alter much of Michele's monologue.

Meanwhile, he continued the search for subjects for two other one-act operas to make up the trilogy. Since Gabriele D'Annunzio and Tristan Bernard had failed to come up with contributions some years previously, he looked to others for assistance. On 29 May 1916, he pressed Adami for ideas: 'You must seriously think of another subject. This is a gadfly that stings me continually. But, for all my thinking and my scrutiny of my thoughts of today and yesterday, nothing emerges that is of any use to me. It is sad, very sad, for time is flying...' He asked Sybil Seligman if she knew 'something specially poetical and lofty'; but it was Giovacchino Forzano, the literary adviser to the judge in the Ouida affair, who came to the rescue. He had interviewed Puccini some years previously for the Florentine newspaper *La nazione*. Before his time as a journalist, he had studied medicine and law, and had briefly tried a singing career as a baritone. Now he lived in Viareggio, not only writing plays and libretti, but also working as a producer at La Scala and the Teatro Reale in Rome. He remembered an idea he had had for a one-act play, *Suor Angelica*. It was the simple tale of a young girl from an aristocratic family, who has been forced to become a nun after having an illegitimate baby.

After seven years without news of her son, she is visited by her unforgiving aunt, the Princess, who tells her that the boy died two years previously. In her grief, Sister Angelica takes poison, hoping to join her child in Heaven, but then, recollecting that suicide is a mortal sin, prays to the Virgin Mary, who appears in a vision with the child to lead her to paradise. The story is very similar to that provided by Salvatore Di Giacomo for Giordano's *Mese Mariano* (1910). There are some parallels too, not only in the plot but also in the orchestration, with *Le Jongleur de Notre-Dame* (Our Lady's Juggler) by Massenet (1902), for which the librettist, Maurice Léna, had used a mediaeval legend from a collection of stories by Anatole France published in 1892. However, *Le Jongleur* is about monks in the Abbey of Cluny, whereas Puccini's story is set in a convent – his only opera to have an entirely female cast.

Forzano wrote a scenario, with which Puccini was immediately taken, as the librettist later recalled:

I did not know that he had a sister who was a nun. The subject pleased him very much indeed. The finale – in which the nun drinks the juice of poisonous herbs in order to see her son again in Heaven – moved him. He told me to begin writing the verses and hurried to Milan to tell the publisher, Tito Ricordi, about it. After two days, he wrote to me, still with the usual humorous Tuscan simplicity: 'I told Tito angelically about the poison in the salad herbs and the rain of gold pieces, and he was bowled over. I'll write again tomorrow. It's cold here and dark by seven o'clock; you bump into the passers-by because the lights are not as golden as in Sister Angelica's little church of Cellole. I am now indifferent to everything that is not angelic.'

The reasons why it appealed to Giacomo are obvious. The

1922 stage designs by Bozetto del Rovescalli for *Suor Angelica*.

147

plea for compassion and forgiveness to an unforgiving world by someone who has committed 'a sin of the flesh' was one with which he could identify. Here too was the pathos he had asked D'Annunzio to supply. The religion of his previous heroine, Minnie, was of the bible-punching variety, appropriate to the Wild West setting. She was prepared to cheat at cards and beat the hangman to achieve her own ends, however desirable her wish to redeem Dick Johnson. But in Sister Angelica there is the pleading sweetness of Cio-Cio-San, combined with the flawed character that the composer appeared to find so irresistible in real and fictional women.

Puccini often visited his eldest sister, Iginia, at her Convent at Vicopelago near Lucca, where she was now Mother Superior, and this gave him access to authentic detail and atmosphere. It is said that he played and sang the completed opera to the sisters, and many of them were deeply moved by it. He was not himself religious, though the dramatic possibilities of Catholic ceremonies fascinated him. In the estimation of his friend, Father Panichelli, Puccini was an unbeliever. The priest did, however, assist Giacomo once more, by finding the Latin prayer to be sung as a hymn by the celestial chorus during the 'miracle' scene at the end of *Suor Angelica*, which the composer irreverently dubbed the '*Marcia reale della Madonna*' (The Madonna's Royal March). The 'intimate memoir' by the curate of Torre del Lago, Dante del Fiorentino, portrays Puccini as a non-practising man, who was sympathetic to the Church, though the gushing, anecdotal style of the book makes it a generally unreliable source. Fiorentino did manage to get a contribution of 500 lire out of the composer for a new bell for the church, contrary to the expectations of some in the village, and commented in his memoir:

He delighted in bells, and he delighted in all the sounds of the country. In *Madama Butterfly* you can hear the robins making their nests, an effect which he produces by a succession of seconds, played by the oboes and flutes, and followed by muted violins, *con sordina*, in octaves. In *The Girl of the Golden West* [sic], when Harry tells the story of how David killed Goliath with the jawbone of an ass, as the instruments leap from one high note to another, you can hear the braying of the ass. It is the same in *Il tabarro* where Frugola extols the beauty of the Persian cat – the oboes provide the meowing of the cat. In *Suor Angelica* he imitates the bleating of the lamb, in *Gianni Schicchi* a whole orchestra of birds, and in *Madama Butterfly* you hear the frogs croaking as the maestro heard them along the Burlamacca Canal between Lake Massaciuccoli and the sea.

He might have added that in *Suor Angelica* Puccini also portrayed the bird to which two sisters stop and listen although they are late for prayers, the wasps that sting Sister Chiara, and the donkey that carries donated supplies into the convent.

At about this time, Puccini was in the habit of carrying a pocket-sized copy of *La Divinia Commedia* (The Divine Comedy) by Dante Alighieri (1265-1321) to read on his many train journeys. He had certainly considered it previously as a source of a trilogy of operas related to its main sections – *Inferno*, *Purgatorio* and *Paradiso*, but the idea had not come to fruition. It is uncertain whether it was Puccini himself, or Forzano, who first suggested the story of Gianni Schicchi from the *Inferno* of *La Divinia Commedia*. This wily Florentine of the thirteenth century uses his gift of mimicry to impersonate a wealthy land-owner, Buoso Donati, who has just died and left all his money to a monastery. The 'bereaved' relatives enlist the help of Schicchi, whose daughter Lauretta can only marry the man she loves (Rinuccio, a distant relative of Donati), if she has a dowry. Schicchi reminds the relatives of the perils of forging a will – exile from their beloved Florence and amputation of the right hand. He then dresses up as Donati and dictates a new will to a notary, giving the relatives some of what each wants, but leaving the three most coveted items – the best mule in Tuscany, the house, and the mills at Signa – to 'my devoted and affectionate friend, Gianni Schicchi'. The aghast relatives can do nothing. Gianni kicks them out of what is now *his* house, Lauretta and Rinuccio declare their love, and Schicchi points out to the audience that, though Dante placed him in hell, there were extenuating circumstances, which may excuse his actions in their eyes. Puccini encapsulated the plot in one of his pieces of doggerel:

> *S'apre la scena col morto in casa.*
> *Tutt'i parenti borbottan preci*
> *viene quel Gianni – tabula rasa*
> *fiorini d'oro divetan ceci.*

> (Up goes the curtain, the rich man is dead,
> The relatives, praying, are all round the bed.
> Gianni, arriving, soon spots what's afoot,
> And quickly makes off with their hopes of the loot.)

On receiving Forzano's scenario, the composer was so pleased with it that he set aside his 'new nun', as he called *Suor Angelica*, with the intention of starting work at once on *Gianni Schicchi*, as he announced to his librettist in another verse:

149

Dopo Il tabarro *di tinta nera*
sento la voglia di buffeggiare.
Lei non si picchi
se faccio prima quel Gianni Schicchi.

(After the black tones portrayed in *The Cloak*
I think I deserve a bit of a joke.
So please don't think me absurdly cheeky,
If I begin first on *Gianni Schicchi*.)

Yet he did not find it as easy as he had expected to escape from the dark colours of the one opera to the light comedy of the other. 'I fear that ancient Florence does not suit me,' he confided to Adami, 'nor is it a subject that would appeal much to the public at large; because I write for all races of men!' So he returned to *Suor Angelica*, completing it on 14 September 1917, then finishing *Gianni Schicchi* on 20 April 1918. The composer's failing eyesight does not seem to have slowed him up, though he now wrote on music manuscript paper with well-spaced staves and in pencil instead of ink. His unusual speed of composition was due not only to wartime travel restrictions, but also to good collaboration with his librettist, who, because he was working on his own original material, had the freedom to meet Puccini's exacting wishes much more easily than his predecessors. Since Forzano lived close by at Viareggio, there was little need for them to correspond, so, apart from their exchange of doggerel, there is no record of how extensive their discussions and alterations were. Sadly, these two one-act operas are the only results of this potentially

1922 stage designs for
Il trittico.

150

excellent partnership.

In their *Giacomo Puccini intimo*, published two years after the composer's death, his friends Marotti and Pagni recounted how a group of them, including Forzano, engaged in what might now be called a 'brainstorming session' to find the right word to suggest a trilogy. Eventually Marotti came up with *Trittico* (Triptych), the word used for a three-panelled picture, especially an altar piece. Although they knew that this suggested a greater connection between the three than was justified, the title stuck, and there is no doubt that it expresses the complementary nature of the three operas – a dark, violent melodrama, a sentimental and pious morality play, and a sparkling comedy.

Comparisons had already been made between Puccini's music and that of Debussy, and some critics were to draw similar parallels after hearing *Il trittico*, particularly *Il tabarro* and *Suor Angelica*. The French composer died on 25 March 1918 in Paris, which prompted Puccini to write to the *Giornale d'Italia* a month later:

When today I hear people speak of Debussyism, as if it were a system to follow or not to follow, I should like to tell these young musicians of the doubts which, as I can attest from my personal knowledge, assailed the great artist in his later years. His harmonic procedures, which, when they were first made known, appeared so surprising and full of a new beauty, became less and less so in the course of time, until ultimately they surprised no one. Even to the composer himself they appeared to represent a restricted field of experiment, and, I repeat, I know how much he attempted, in vain, to escape from this field. A fervent admirer of Debussy, I was anxiously awaiting to see how Debussy himself proposed to revolt against Debussyism. Now the great artist is dead, and we cannot know the manner, possibly very beneficial, in which he would have carried out this revolt.

It is not surprising that Puccini fulminated against those who tried to categorise Debussy's music as a 'system', or who pointed out the technical ways in which Puccini's music owed a debt to Debussy, by the use of various harmonic and stylistic technical devices. What Puccini's music (from *La bohème*, or even *Manon Lescaut*, onwards) shared with that of Debussy and Massenet, was the delicate sensibility that frequently sets the nerve ends tingling – transparent, subtle and restrained orchestration, conveying the exquisite, yet fragile, pleasure of the finely-observed moment, mixed with the piquancy of anticipated loss, that is so much a characteristic of the *fin de siècle* artist.

Like millions of other people, Giacomo and Sybil shared

anxieties about their sons involved in the War – Tonio was at the Front, Vincent Seligman in Salonica – both were to survive. In Italy, sadly, more people were killed by the epidemic of Spanish influenza that broke out in the autumn of 1918 than in the First World War. Torre del Lago, for instance, lost 15 in the War and 80 from the 'flu. But earlier, on 8 June, before the end of the War, Puccini wrote to Sybil:

I have had your dear letters – but what a terrible thing this War is! God will that it may be as you say, that it will soon be over! Everything is paralysed, but don't let's talk about my art – I've finished the three operas, and they're going to be given for the first time in New York in November. The manager and conductor are coming over to see me; at present they're in New York, but they are going to make the journey on purpose to arrange things with me. I should dearly have loved to have heard this new music of mine, and I had hoped that the War would be over in November – but it seems as though we shall never live to see the world set straight again! My health isn't bad – but food is scarce – very little meat, and that only occasionally – the bread is bad – I've still got my diabetes, but it doesn't trouble me much now.

The original idea of mounting the operas in Rome had been abandoned, because too many singers and musicians were serving in the armed forces, so it was agreed to accept the Metropolitan Opera's offer to stage the première in New York. In fact, it took place on 14 December 1918, after the Armistice had been signed on 11 November, but travel was still too difficult for Puccini to be there. It was a bitter disappointment to him. However, the conductor, Roberto Moranzoni, had gone through the score with him at Viareggio, and the manager, Gatti-Casazza, kept him informed by telegram of the progress of the rehearsals. The cast was a strong one. Claudia Muzio, the Italian soprano whose father was manager of Covent Garden and the Metropolitan Opera in his time, created the rôle of Giorgetta in *Il tabarro*, Geraldine Farrar sang Suor Angelica, and Giuseppe De Luca, the baritone from Rome who had created the rôle of Sharpless, was the first Gianni Schicchi. Each opera was cheered, and there were 40 curtain calls, but it was the comedy that won most praise, while *Suor Angelica*, which Puccini himself favoured as the best of the three, had a lukewarm reception.

The next day, the critic of *The New York Herald* concluded: 'I cannot think that, from his own standpoint, in these operas Mr Puccini has given us anything markedly new, and yet he has said a good many old things in a new way, and his score abounds with orchestral quips and oddities, pictorially characteristic, orchestrally effective, and dramatically descriptive and appropriate.' *The New York Times* wrote *Suor Angelica* off as 'sugary...mock-Maeterlinck...mock-turtle mysticism...and all insincere', pointing out that it contained only one rôle, 'which was played with histrionic beauty by Geraldine Farrar, who, luckily, was in better voice than usual.' But the same critic was full of praise for *Gianni Schicchi*: 'The gaiety is irresistible, and the music as frothing and exhilarating as champagne.' This view was shared by *The Tribune* reviewer who wrote: 'This comedy is so uproariously funny, the music so full of life, humour, and ingenious devices...it was received with uproarious delight, signs of appreciation not waiting till the closing of the curtain.'

The first European production was given at the Teatro Costanzi in Rome on 11 January 1919. The King and Queen were present, but again it was *Gianni Schicchi* that was singled out as 'a little masterpiece' and 'an almost perfect opera'. Puccini hoped for an early performance at Covent Garden, but disagreements over who was to conduct led to a postponement until the next season. Puccini did not want Toscanini, as they were still not reconciled after their quarrel. Instead, he suggested Thomas Beecham, but the management would not agree, so Covent Garden re-opened on 12 May 1919 with the Royal Family hearing Nellie Melba as Mimi in *La bohème*.

Nevertheless, Giacomo still went to London in June 1919, glad to be able to travel and to see Sybil again. Vincent Seligman painted a verbal picture of him on this visit:

He seemed to have changed but little during the long interval since we had seen him last; his hair had begun to turn white, but it was as abundant as ever; his movements were perhaps a little slower and more measured, but the oncoming of old age, over which he continually laments in his letters, was with him a very gradual and almost imperceptible process, and no one would have guessed that he had turned sixty; and he looked, as he always did until a few months before his death, the very picture of health.

Above all, he had retained that simple boyish outlook on life, that keen appreciation and enjoyment of its 'little things' which never deserted him. Back in his beloved London, he was exactly like a schoolboy on the first few days after term; he must go everywhere and see everything – and all that he saw delighted him.

His wardrobe had become 'sadly depleted' during the War, so he was delighted to shop for clothes. Sybil remarked that he took two hours to walk from one end of Bond Street to the other, because he spent so much time window-shopping. On one occasion, he bought ties of the Brigade of Guards, the Old

153

Etonians, Old Harrovians, the Rifle Brigade and the Royal Artillery, in spite of Vincent's protests, and then taunted him by wearing the Royal Artillery tie for lunch at the Savoy. 'I offered up a silent prayer,' Vincent confessed, 'that no one would notice it...and I fancied that the famous twinkle in his eye was rather more pronounced than usual.'

He went to the theatre several times, including *Chu Chin Chow*, which had been an enormous hit during the War. It did not seem to have made much impression on Puccini, except that he noticed an elderly gentleman with a score in the front row 'conducting away by himself as though he were at a Bayreuth festival', so he joined in too from the stage box. On his way back to Italy, he met Tito Ricordi, who had moved to Paris after being forced to resign from the family firm. Puccini hinted to the Seligmans that this had probably come about because his attempts to sponsor new talent had led to disastrous

154

losses for the firm. 'It made me rather unhappy to see him,' Puccini wrote to Sybil. 'Now he's thinking of going into the cinema business!' However, it was a chance to make peace after their previous disagreements. Although he felt that Tito had been fairly unpleasant to him, the composer was sorry to see such a long family tradition end in this way. In fact, Tito's plans did not work out and he fell on hard times. One of the two people put in charge of the firm was an old friend of Puccini, Carlo Clausetti, who would be with him in the last days of his life.

The delayed first performance of *Il trittico* at Covent Garden was eventually scheduled for 18 June 1920, so Puccini and Forzano returned to supervise rehearsals. It was during these that a young cellist in the orchestra, John Barbirolli, later to achieve fame as a conductor, was amused to notice that the composer wore an Old Etonian tie. King George V and Queen Mary were present at the first night, though it was reported that they arrived after the performance of *Il tabarro* – possibly because they had been warned of its subject matter. The audience greeted the operas enthusiastically, but *The Times* sagely remarked: 'They could hardly be anything but a success at the present moment, when their composer is so much the darling of the opera-going public that half, at least, of the present season has been devoted to the repetition of his earlier works.' He was given numerous curtain calls after each opera. 'It was,' said *The Times*, 'a unique chance to offer him the personal tribute of thanks.' In reality, *Suor Angelica* was withdrawn after two performances, on the excuse that the soprano was ill and no replacement could be found, while *Gianni Schicchi* was

One of Puccini's motor cars – he had a fanatical obsession with cars and speedboats.

155

hailed as 'a gem, a masterpiece of comic opera'. In January 1921, Puccini was still telling Sybil that he thought *Suor Angelica* 'the *best* of the three operas', but it is significant that Ricordi's were now giving permission for the other two to be performed without it. Puccini had heard Lotte Lehmann sing *Suor Angelica* in Vienna the previous October, but few, if any, could bring the depth and poignancy that she brought to the rôle. He described her ass 'a fine, delicate artist – simple and without any of the airs of a prima donna, with a voice as sweet as honey.' Yet, after the performance of the complete *Il trittico* at Lucca later in the year, Puccini came to realise that the wise old man Giulio Ricordi had been right all the time – the three one-act operas were too long to be given together.

On his return from London, Puccini found 'a strike on, which was half a revolution, on account of the high cost of living', and he was worried that he might lose the use of his car. There was a great deal of unrest in Italy after the Armistice. The Italians felt they had been unfairly treated by the Allies at the Treaty of Versailles in 1919, although they had gained the important port of Trieste, improved their frontier with the annexation of the South Tyrol, and seen the destruction of their traditional enemy, the Habsburg monarchy. Nevertheless, the myth of the 'mutilated peace' appeared to have won almost universal acceptance. It was exploited by none other than Gabriele D'Annunzio. In September 1919, with 2,000 army deserters, he occupied the town of Fiume on the Adriatic, which the Italians had always coveted. This act was to be mirrored in countless ways throughout disaffected Italy: peasants occupied land and workers took over factories; but

The Fascists' March on Rome, 24 October 1922.

156

Benito Mussolini with
Vittorio Emanuele III, King
of Italy, in 1923.

the Socialists failed either to deal with, or to mobilise, the
discontent. Instead, they split into several parties, including the
Italian Communist Party, formed specifically on the advice of
Lenin. 'Italy is really in a bad way,' Puccini stated in July 1920.
He was so disillusioned that he contemplated leaving his
homeland altogether. When the Fascists' March on Rome in
October 1922 forced the King to ask Mussolini to form a
government, Puccini was among those who welcomed *il duce*,
because he would restore order after the chaos. 'God grant, he
is the man we need!', he wrote to Adami. 'He is welcome if he
will reform our country and give it a little peace!' Although he
did not profess to belong to any political party, Puccini was
made an honourary member of the Fascist Party, and, in 1924,
a *Senatore del regno* (Senator of the Realm), which he laugh-
ingly called *Sonatore del Regno* (Player of the Realm). As with
his attitude towards Germany at the beginning of the War, his

157

political judgment appeared to many to be decidedly suspect.

It is possible that the discontent that had spread into rural communities was partly responsible for Puccini's move from his beloved Torre del Lago to Viareggio. Dante del Fiorentino related how, when he was once crossing the Lake with Puccini in his motorboat, a fisherman shook his fist at him, and shouted: 'It's yours now; soon it will be ours!' On reaching home, the shaken composer said: 'There's a new spirit strangling Italy. There is a mortal sickness spreading through the world, and it has even come to our peaceful Tuscany. I have never intentionally done anyone harm. I've tried to make people happy. Then why should that man hate me? There was hatred in his voice and in his face.' A more immediate reason may well have been that a peat factory was being constructed near by, causing much local resentment. The Lake was being dredged, and the noise and the smell were unbearable. Puccini had bought a plot of land at Viareggio at the time of his relationship with Josephine, and so in 1919 he started to build a villa there. He did not like the town much, but it was near the sea, and was not then the crowded resort it is today. Viareggio's other claim to fame is that Shelley's body had been washed up there and cremated in the presence of Byron.

The house was set in a large garden filled with pine trees, though Elvira complained of the lack of air, so, two years after they moved there in 1922, Puccini had 12 of them cut down – 'though it grieves my heart to do it,' he told Adami. His study was connected by a small staircase to his bedroom, so that he did not disturb the household when working late. It was spacious, with an uninterrupted view of the Mediterranean,

Puccini on Lake Massaciuccoli in one of his motorboats.

158

Puccini in his specially-designed study in Viareggio, working on *Turandot*.

and furnished with a Steinway grand, two leather armchairs, several tables on which he could spread his music sheets, a large sofa, and a fireplace, over which he had mounted some of his stuffed hunting trophies. With his 'boyish outlook on life', as Vincent Seligman called it, he had many modern gadgets installed, like the concealed button on the brass plaque at the entrance gate that, when pressed, caused the gate to glide open. There were also water pipes up into the treetops, that created artificial rain, which was used to water the garden.

Although he had been reluctant to leave Torre, he became attached to this house, and, whether for this reason, or because of advancing years, became less keen to travel. One result was that discussions with his librettists about his next, and last, opera, were all conducted by letter, so that the trail that led to his masterpiece, *Turandot*, is especially well documented.

Chapter 10

Still Alive and Unconquered

All the music I have written so far seems to me just a farce in comparison with the music I now write. (Puccini six months before his death, in an undated letter to Adami about *Turandot*.)

The success of their comedy *Gianni Schicchi* encouraged Puccini and Forzano to cast around for another comic subject. 'I feel the proper spirit coursing through my veins,' Puccini wrote to the playwright, 'and I cherish now, and tomorrow and after that, the idea of an opera that will uncork the fountain of a spring that I feel pressing inside me...' Forzano was working on a play *Cristoforo Sly*, based on the drunken tailor in the Prologue to Shakespeare's *The Taming of the Shrew*, and so, with Puccini's agreement, he began to adapt it as an opera. That the composer was not wholly committed to the idea is revealed by a counter-proposal that he made about an opera based on fairy tales set in the hills surrounding Lucca. A year later – in July 1920 – Puccini announced to Sybil: '*Sly* is no good. Forzano is unhappy about it, and so am I – for his sake. But what can I do?' Although he debated waiting to see the play in the theatre, he wrote to an old friend from Lucca, Carlo Paladini: 'Forzano has prepared a dish that was too sumptuous, and it was obvious to me from the beginning that it was indigestible.' Forzano's play went on to achieve considerable success in Italy, and was used as the basis for an opera by Wolf-Ferrari in 1927, which was not particularly well received.

In the end, Puccini's thoughts about the hills near Lucca led to the genesis of a 'fairy tale' opera of a rather different kind to the one he originally had in mind. Nestling in the environs was the popular summer resort of Bagni di Lucca, where Giacomo spent some time in the years following the War. It was here that he renewed his acquaintance with the scholarly Renato Simoni, who, after many years as drama critic for *Il corriere della sera*,

Puccini in his later years.

161

had succeeded Giacosa as editor of *La Lettura*. He was a noted playwright and historian of the theatre, having also written the libretto for Umberto Giordano's *Madame Sans-Gêne*, as well as several for Giulio Ricordi. Puccini thought that he might well be the collaborator who could inspire Adami to higher things, so he asked them both to prepare a libretto based on *Oliver Twist*, which he had seen in a stage adaptation by Beerbohm Tree during one of his recent visits to London. They decided to concentrate on the character of Nancy, the companion of Bill Sikes amidst the poverty of back-street, criminal life in Victorian London, who, in trying to help Oliver, is brutally murdered by her lover. The appeal of such a heroine to Puccini was obvious; yet, in the spring of 1920, he rejected it, after the collaborators had produced a versified first act and detailed scenarios for the last two acts.

It may be that its similarity to elements of the plots of *La bohème*, *La fanciulla del West* and *Il tabarro* discouraged him, but it is more probable that by then he had been diverted by another idea. He had been paying one of his flying visits to Milan and met Adami and Simoni for lunch in a restaurant before catching a train. Simoni suddenly suggested that they might look at something by the eighteenth-century Venetian playwright, Carlo Gozzi, about whose life he had himself written a play. 'A fairy-tale,' Adami recalled him saying, 'which would perhaps be the synthesis of his other typical fables? I don't know...something fantastic and remote, interpreted with human sentiment and presented in modern colours?' Puccini then remembered having been told about Max Reinhardt's Berlin production of Gozzi's *Turandot* (1762) in a German adaptation by Karl Vollmöller. Busoni had written the incidental music, and then a short opera, *Turandot*, first performed in Zürich in 1917. Puccini's former teacher, Bazzini, had written a *Turanda*, while Giacosa had used it in his verse-drama *Il trionfo d'amore*, so there were many connections to bring it to his mind. The Gozzi play was based on a French version of a tale of ancient China from *A Thousand and One Nights*, about the cruel Princess Turandot, whose heart is ice, and who asks three riddles of each suitor. The penalty for failure is death by beheading. Calaf, a foreign prince, solves the riddles, but she refuses him, so he sets her the riddle of discovering his name, triumphing when her icy heart melts and she realises that his name is Love. It was immensely popular in Italy and much performed. Simoni rushed back to his apartment to get a copy of an Italian translation of the German adaptation by Schiller, which he handed to Puccini through the train window. On 18 March 1920, after reading it, the composer wrote back from Rome, where he was attending the second production of *Il trittico*. He was already full of ideas:

We should reduce the number of acts, and we should strive to make it slim and effective, and, above all, heighten the passion of Turandot, who has for so long been buried in the ashes of her immense pride... Turandot as seen through a modern mentality: yours, Adami's, and mine... To sum up, I am of the opinion that *Turandot* is the most normal and most human of all Gozzi's plays.

With his usual initial enthusiasm, Puccini encouraged his collaborators to see 'what a beautiful and original work' it could be 'and how fascinating'. He urged them to put all the resources of their hearts and heads into creating 'something which will make the world weep'. He urged Adami to make Gozzi's *Turandot* his basis, 'but on that you must rear another figure; I mean – I can't explain! From our imaginations (and we shall need them) there must arise so much that is beautiful and attractive and gracious as to make our story a *bouquet* of success.' He clearly sensed the need for the addition of a contrasting female character like Liù. Meanwhile, he went in search of background colour, reading about old Chinese music, obtaining scenic material from Reinhardt's production, and getting drawings of instruments that could be used on the stage. It may have been through one of his London friends that he obtained copies of some fragments of ancient Chinese music, possibly from the British Museum. He was able to hear some at the home of his friend, Baron Fassini-Camossi at Bagni di Lucca, when he was there with the two librettists in 1920. From his years in China as a member of the Italian consular service, the Baron had a fine collection of Chinese *objets d'art*, that included an old musical-box which played two tunes, one being the Imperial Hymn. Puccini was to use both in his opera.

His dependency on librettists had always irked him, and he especially disliked the period of waiting before he could begin composition. Yet this anxiety was also an expression of his own inner doubts about his creative power, and an awareness of his own limitations. He explained this in a perceptive letter to Adami in the spring of 1920:

If I touch the piano, my hands become covered with dust. My desk is piled high with letters – there isn't a trace of music. Music? Useless if I have no libretto. I have the great weakness of being able to write only when my puppet executioners are moving on the scene. If only I could be a purely symphonic writer! I should then at least cheat time...and my public. But that was not for me. I was born so many

163

years ago – oh, so many, too many, almost a century...and Almighty God touched me with His little finger and said: "Write for the theatre – mind, only for the theatre," and I have obeyed the supreme command. Had He marked me out for some other task, perhaps I should not be, as now, without material. O you, who say you are working, while you are really doing something entirely different – films, plays, poetry, articles – and never think, as you ought to think, of the man who has the earth under his feet, and yet who feels the ground receding under him with every hour and every day, as if a landslide would swallow him up! I receive such nice and encouraging letters, but if, instead of these, one act were to arrive of our glittering Princess, don't you think it would be better? You would give me back my calm and my confidence, and the dust would not settle on my piano any more; so much pounding would I do, and my desk would have its sheets of music paper with a thousand staves!

During the last four years of his life, as he wrestled with *Turandot*, his letters betray more than ever a consciousness of the passing of time and the urgency of finishing the opera. Yet he was also torn by a seeming inability to commit himself absolutely to this final act of creation, and many have seen it as a significant insight into his psychology that, ultimately, he could *not* complete it.

Several of his suggestions to the librettists in the early stages were extremely perceptive. Gozzi had included masked characters in the tradition of the Venice Carnivale and the *commedia dell'arte*, which Puccini at first saw as clowns and philosophers, 'who here and there might risk a joke', and he even wondered about cutting them out. But then he saw that they were there to 'bring us back to the reality of our lives', drawing a parallel with Shakespeare's use of Caliban and Trinculo, Ariel and the spirits, to set into perspective the central characters of *The Tempest*. In Puccini's *Turandot* Ping, Pang and Pong speak not only as the voice of the Emperor (they are his Chief Ministers), but also at times as the voice of the observer commenting on the action, reminding the audience about their own feelings as they are touched by the drama.

The first sketches of the music were under way by July 1920, when Puccini went to Vienna for the first productions there of *La rondine* and *Il trittico*, but he found it terribly cold and longed to be home. The journey back was tedious because he missed his connection, so he had to stay overnight in both Venice and Bologna. 'I have carried about with me on all my journeys a large bundle of melancholy,' he wrote to Adami on 10 November. He was acutely aware that he needed to keep the momentum of creativity going, otherwise he would be prey to morbid doubts and fears about his own ability:

I keep thinking that *Turandot* will never be finished. I cannot work like this. When the fever diminishes, it ends by disappearing altogether, and without fever there is no creation, because emotional art is a kind of illness, an exceptional state of mind, an over-excitation of every fibre and every atom of one's being... It is not a matter of just finishing it. One must give lasting life to a thing that must live before it can be born... Will I have the strength to follow you? Who knows? Shall I be tired, mistrustful, weighed down by age and spiritual suffering, by my continual discontent? Who knows? You should work as if you were working for a young man of 30, and I will do my best, and if I do not succeed, it will be my fault.

In December 1920, he was at his new hunting lodge at Torre della Tagliata in the coastal region of the Maremma to the south of Pisa. Whilst he loved its isolation and the superb hunting, he was already having second thoughts about it as a place to which he could retreat to find peace and quiet, because it was so cold and remote that he felt increasingly depressed there. Just before Christmas, Adami arrived to read the libretto of the first act to him. However, the librettists had filled it with so many irrelevant details in order to get an authentic Chinese atmosphere, that the reading lasted an hour. 'It isn't an act,' groaned the composer; 'it's a lecture. Do you think I can possibly put a conference to music?' To Sybil he wrote: 'Adami has brought me a first act that will never do – I'm very much afraid the libretto will never be how I want it.'

By 15 January, things had changed, for he wrote from Milan to Sybil telling her that he had a fine first act, and that he was feeling well 'after my horrible stay in the Maremma'. Sybil and Giacomo met in March on the Riviera, but she had to return home suddenly due to a severe bout of sciatica. The composition seems to have gone well until April, when once again Puccini was waiting for the librettists to produce the second and third acts. The physical symptoms that had so often been associated with periods of difficulty in composition started again, as he related to Sybil on 21 April:

I am not too well; for several days, I've had a pain in my mouth (my teeth), aggravated by bad temper, by lack of faith, by being tired of life – in a word, nothing is right for me...

I'm very, very down. I don't seem to have any more faith in myself; my work terrifies me, and I find nothing good anywhere. I feel as though, from now on, I were finished – and it may well be that this is so; I am old – this is literally the truth – and it's a very sad thing, especially for an artist. [He was 63 years old.]

Yet he could be full of fun in his letters of this time: in one of the many letters he wrote to Adami he referred to the librettists as *attaccaticci-vento-bestie bovine* (sticky-windy-bovine animals) with the explanation: *colla* (glue) – *bora* (north wind) – *tori* (bulls), making up *collaboratori* (collaborators). A few weeks later, however, in June 1921, he was writing to Adami in a very different mood:

Am I utterly forsaken by my beloved brethren in *Turandot*? Not a word – after so many promises, so much communion! I need the second act in a day or two! And I am needing, too, to feel myself loved a little, and, like a faithful dog, to wag my tail. But, as far as you two are concerned, I have a long face and my tail is drooping.

Having completed the first act in August, he began work on Act Two as soon as he had the libretto, but things did not go well. By mid-September he was writing to Simoni: 'That second act! I find no way out; perhaps I torture myself because I have a fixed idea: *Turandot* must be in two acts only. What do you think?' He had tried the same tactic with *La bohème*, as a way of avoiding the need to set words for which he had originally pestered the librettists. Simoni and Adami held out, carrying on with their work on the third act: perhaps they realised that the melting of the ice Princess required the greater space of three acts, in order to be psychologically convincing. By November, he was telling Sybil that '*Turandot* languishes. I haven't got the second act as I want it yet, and I don't feel myself capable any more of composing music.' His despair was increased by a prolonged silence from both the librettists, provoking him to discuss with Forzano the idea of setting his *Chinese Play* instead, into which he could transfer much of the *Turandot* material. By Christmas time, however, he decided that he had got *Turandot* and could not afford to be diverted again.

Forzano at the time of *Il trittico*.

His letter to Sybil had been written in Rome, where he had gone to judge a competition of 25 operas by young composers, only to find that several of the other judges had opted out. He wrote to Adami:

Mascagni is at Pisa conducting his *Marat*. Toscanini has given up for a thousand reasons of his own. Bossi [a composer of organ and chamber music] has his son competing and has therefore made off. Cilea is at Naples. There remain d'Atri, who has given proof of musical judgment...and Rosadi, who hums the Masses of my eighteenth-century ancestor... *Ergo* I am not plucking this bird!

Meanwhile, the press had latched onto the disagreements between composer and librettists to the fury of the latter; but

166

Giacomo told Sybil, in his first letter to her from his new home at Viareggio, two days before Christmas 1921: 'I wasn't satisfied with this libretto and I said so... and now they've recognised how wrong they were, and are going to work enthusiastically along the lines of my suggestions.' By the spring of 1922, he was well into the composition of Act Two, most comfortable in his new house, and pleased that 'all the world over, my operas still hold their own' with the gratifying result that he was receiving a continuous and substantial flow of royalties. Furthermore, the manager of Covent Garden passed a message to Puccini, through Sybil, drawing his attention to the fact that Ricordi's in New York had published a ragtime dance made up of 'the most popular airs in Puccini's operas'. The matter was settled out of court by substantial damages, with which the composer may well have bought his 'marvellous new car, an eight-cylinder limousine Lancia' and a motor-boat that did 'over 25 miles an hour'.

By early July 1922, he had received the words for Act Three, which he found good in parts, though he told Adami they would need to be cut considerably. He asked the librettists to allow time for 'the icy demeanour of Turandot to melt in the course of the duet'. Although he had stressed earlier that he did not want 'too much psychology', he was aware that the change in the Princess had to be as credible as possible. Before beginning work again, he went on a motoring tour round Europe with Tonio and several friends, visiting Germany, Holland and Switzerland. He was reported to have been in high spirits throughout the trip. However, on 28 August, when they were staying at Ingolstadt in Bavaria, a goose bone became stuck in his throat. It caused him much pain, so a doctor was called to remove it. He made light of it, punning on the place name 'in gola sta' (it sticks in the throat), but, after his death from throat cancer two years later, some thought that this incident might have caused the disease.

It was scarcely surprising that one of the qualities Puccini had been looking for in the *Turandot* libretto was a 'sympathetic understanding of human grief', which he had explored in previous operas, and which was ever present in his consciousness. In October 1922, after his return from holiday, it was again brought to the forefront of his mind by the death of his sister, Iginia. He wrote to a friend: 'Poor little nun, she died with my name on her lips. Thus the Puccinis depart, little by little. It is very sad to witness the death of those we love, and those who remain await the great journey, which is, perhaps, less terrible than we think.' In March 1923, he penned another piece of doggerel verse, that was not found until after his death, but which expresses the pervading melancholy that was so much a part of his psychological make-up:

I feel alone, without a friend,
Even music makes me sad.
When death shall come to find me
I shall be glad to rest.
Oh, how hard is my life,
Though I seem happy to many.
But what of my successes?
They pass and what remains?
It's worth so little –
They are ephemeral things.
Life runs on towards the abyss.
Those who are alive and young are happy,
But who is aware of all this?
One's youth passes quickly,
And the eye scrutinises eternity.

As if he needed reminding of the inevitability of death, many of his relatives, friends and associates had died in recent years. Of his librettists, Fontana and Illica had both died in 1919. 'Poor Illica! Another friend gone!' he wrote to Adami. 'One

Arrigo Boito at work in his study towards the end of his life, with a portrait of Verdi hanging on the wall behind him.

168

Caruso with his wife, Dorothy, and daughter, Gloria, leaving America for the last time on board the *S.S. Presidente Wilson* on 28 May 1921.

after another, a sad catalogue that goes on lengthening piti-lessly! We have to resign ourselves, but one chafes all the same. What a life!' Amongst famous friends in opera, there had not only been Giulio Ricordi, but also Boito in 1918, Leoncavallo the following year and then, tragically, Caruso died of pleurisy in Naples. His American doctors were blamed for a wrong diagnosis, and it was treated as such a national catastrophe that the King of Italy allowed the royal basilica of San Francesco di Paola, only previously opened for royal baptisms, weddings and funerals, to be used for Caruso's funeral.

By November, though the first act was finished, Puccini was complaining to Adami that 'there isn't a ray to pierce the gloom which shrouds the rest. Perhaps it is wrapped for ever in impenetrable darkness. I have the feeling that I shall have to put this work on one side.' Consequently, he used two of his familiar tactics to avoid the difficulties: he revived the idea of merging the last two acts into one, and he began to discuss alternative operas with Adami. Although they agreed to look at an eighteenth-century Venetian subject, Puccini returned to working on the three-act *Turandot*, and, in particular to the rôle of the slave-girl, Liù, who is in love with Calaf. Her unas-suming, quiet devotion may possibly have been linked uncon-sciously in his mind with that simple, tragic servant girl of his own household, Doria Manfredi. Liù did not appear in Gozzi:

169

she was a creation of the composer and librettists, a contrast to the Princess, a typically tragic Puccini heroine. On 3 November, he wrote to Adami: 'I believe that Liù must sacrifice herself because of some sorrow, but I don't see how this can be developed, unless we make her die under torture. And why not? Her death could be an element in softening the heart of the Princess.' This was the origin of the compelling scene in which the slave girl commits suicide rather than betray Calaf by revealing his name. Yet her death affects neither Calaf, who has admittedly not been in love with her, nor the Princess, with the consequence that the explanation for Turandot's change of heart appears weak. If Liù's death had been partly responsible for this, Puccini could have avoided the Princess's weak aria at the end, which is included only to justify her psychological motivation.

During 1922, Puccini had written to Simoni, complaining that Toscanini 'persists in being my enemy. And why? Who knows! I would, of course, like peace, but he wants to maintain the hostilities.' However, after Christmas 1922, the management of La Scala decided to mount a new production of *Manon Lescaut* conducted by Toscanini. By this time, the two must have already made their peace privately, because they now amicably discussed the score at Viareggio and the composer felt the greatest pleasure in attending rehearsals. He told a friend: 'Never, never have I so enjoyed listening to my music.' After the performance, the critic of *Il corriere della sera* claimed that Puccini had substantially revised it, so the composer wrote to the newspaper pointing out that, apart from 'some modifications in colouring' it was the same as it was 30 years ago: 'When Arturo Toscanini, with the faith and love which ignite the fires of his marvellous art, takes the scalpel and cuts away all the ugliness and brings the work back to its natural state, revealing the composer's true intentions to the public, the old work seems new to the public, and it seems changed. No, it is simply the same work brought to life by the greatest re-creator the musical world boasts.' Toscanini had become artistic director of La Scala in December 1921, so Puccini went on to praise the achievements of his first year in the post:

What he has accomplished at La Scala is marvellous. I travel from theatre to theatre all over the world, and I see and study what is being done elsewhere. I think it is now time to say that what is done at La Scala today is not done in any other theatre. Toscanini has not only been an organiser; he has created an institution, which is the pride of Italian art; for all he has done, he has done out of his love for the opera of Italian artists.

Toscanini conducting at
La Scala in a drawing by
G. Tabet, 1928.

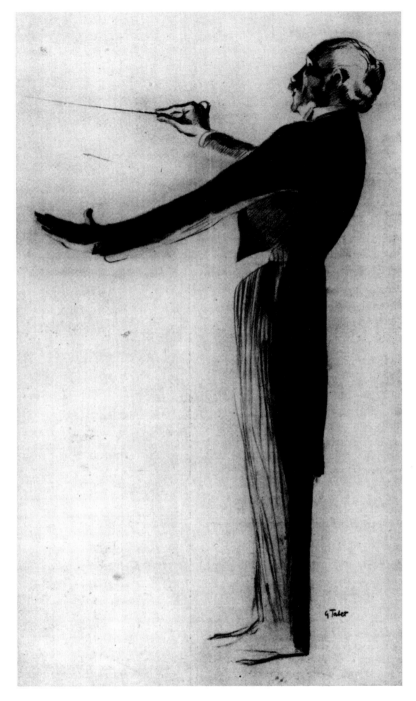

The reconciliation was complete. On 1 February 1923, a
gala performance was given to celebrate the 30th anniversary
of the première of *Manon Lescaut*, and was followed by a
banquet for nearly 500 guests in the composer's honour. 'At
last Milan has honoured me!' he said to Sybil. The next day, he
wrote to Toscanini:

171

You have given me the greatest satisfaction of my life.

In your wonderful interpretation, *Manon* became a far better work than I had thought in those far-off days – you performed this music of mine with such poetic feeling, such *souplesse* and irresistible passion.

Last night I truly felt the greatness of your soul and all your affection for your old friend and companion of those early struggles.

I am happy because you showed, above all, such an understanding for the spirit of my passionate youth of 30 years ago! My beloved creature in the hands of Arturo Toscanini! I thank you from the depth of my heart!

The Vienna State Opera held a Puccini festival in May, so the composer drove there in his new Lancia with Tonio and a friend to see performances of *Butterfly*, *La bohème* and *Tosca*. The last, with the Czech soprano Maria Jeritza, he classed as 'sublime! A mad success! over 500 curtain calls!', but the scheduled performance of *Manon Lescaut* with Lotte Lehmann was postponed until October, so he returned again for that. His visits to Vienna impressed on him the importance of 'a good and permanent opera house', prompting him to write several times to Sybil about the need for such an opera house in London. He also sought an audience with Mussolini to suggest a National Opera House in Rome, but the dictator dismissed the idea peremptorily.

Throughout 1923, work on *Turandot* continued fitfully, though Puccini had finally settled on three acts. At times, he was filled with his usual self-doubt. 'Maybe, or even without the maybe, I am no longer any good,' he wrote to Adami. 'I am a poor, very unhappy man, discouraged, old, useless and disheartened.' He and Elvira were leading a comfortable life at Viareggio, as he told Adami: 'Elvira and I are here, the two *ancêtres*, like two old family portraits frowning from time to time at the cobwebs which tickle us. We sleep, eat, read *Il corriere*, and, with a note or two in the evening, the old composer keeps himself alive.' In June, he began work on Act Three. He had had the outline libretto for a year, but was still waiting for the verses – his letters constantly badger the 'collaborators' to send him more completed verses. Significantly, he was so moved by Liù's death scene, that he wrote the music before receiving the verses. He sent Adami some suggested words to demonstrate the metre, and these were used with little alteration. He did much the same with the Trio of the Masks in Act Two, in order to give the sound of the words an authentic Chinese colour. The orchestration of the second act was completed in February 1924, and he began working on the scoring of the final act, though the librettists had still not produced satisfactory words for the love duet: he had already rejected four versions. It was, in his eyes, absolutely crucial, and he appeared to be both fascinated and paralysed by it. 'The duet! the duet! It is the nodal point, all that is beautiful and vivid in the drama converges on it!'

By March 1924, the opera had been completed apart from the last two scenes, and Puccini wrote to Sybil that he was at work on the duet, which was difficult, 'but I shall end by doing it.' He was still waiting for words for the final duet, although he had been promised them 'within a few days' at the end of January. His correspondence had been mainly with Adami, but now he penned a tactful letter to Simoni:

It is a long time since I have written to you, and since we have written to each other. I have been working desperately for four months and am almost at the end; I lack only the final duet. All the rest is orchestrated... I have put my whole soul into this opera; we shall see, therefore, if my vibrations synchronise with those of the public.

Your duet had good things in it, but it was not sufficiently varied and rapid; Adami and I have worked on it together and it seems to me successfully, especially in its various stages. Since I am coming to Milan, we can go over it again, if only to give it more touches of imagery and some more 'Chinese' details. But I have wanted it to be a human thing, and when the heart speaks, whether it be in China or Holland, the sense is all the same and the purpose is that of all people.

Yet in late May he was telling Sybil: 'I've done no more work, *Turandot* lies here, unfinished. But I *will* finish it – only just at present I've got no desire to work.' On 1 April, he had gone to Florence to hear Arnold Schoenberg conduct his *Pierrot Lunaire* in the Pitti Palace. He had always followed and tried to understand modern music, so he listened attentively to the performance, which, unfortunately, was booed. Puccini was the only musician present who bothered to go backstage to congratulate the composer and discuss the work with him. Schoenberg later wrote:

I take it to have been the expert judges, not the art-lovers, who received my *Pierrot Lunaire* with such hostility when I performed it in Italy. I was indeed honoured that Puccini, not an expert judge, but a practical expert, made a six-hour journey to hear my work, and afterwards said some very friendly things to me. That was good, strange though my music may have remained to him.

A month later, Puccini and Toscanini again fell out. The conductor and Vincenzo Tommasini had completed Boito's

173

Nerone – left unfinished at his death. Puccini had spoken disparagingly of it, and, when he went to attend the dress rehearsal at the end of April, he was devastated to find that Toscanini had left orders for him to be refused admittance. Eventually, on 4 August, he wrote Arturo a long letter blaming a troublemaker for spreading a false report of his comments on *Nerone*, but they were not reconciled for a further month, until Toscanini went to Viareggio to discuss the first production of *Turandot*. Puccini wrote immediately to Adami: 'Toscanini has just left here. We are in perfect and sympathetic agreement, and finally I can breathe. And so the nightmare that has been looming since April is over... The little that I played for Toscanini made a very good impression.' Yet the final duet and finale still remained uncompleted, and he was anxious about it. He told Adami in the same letter:

We discussed the duet, which he [Toscanini] did not like much. What is to be done? I don't know. Toscanini will perhaps ask you and Simoni to come to Salso[maggiore]. I'll come too and we shall see if a way can be found to remedy the situation. I see only darkness before me. I already feel like a blockhead [the Italian is literally: 'I have grown an elephant's head'] about this duet. Speak to Renato [Simoni] about it as well. And we must get out of this difficulty, because I am at my last gasp...

A week or two later, he wrote again to Adami, stressing that this was the point where words and music must move into another dimension: 'It must be a great duet. These two beings, who stand, so to speak, outside the world, are transformed into human beings through love, and this love must take possession of everybody on the stage in an orchestral peroration.' The proposed meeting at Salsomaggiore took place, and, on 8 October, the composer received the verses from Simoni and told Adami that 'they are really beautiful; they round off and justify the duet.' He also met Toscanini and Simoni in a rehearsal room at La Scala and played them those parts of the opera they had not already heard. Arturo was much distressed to see the composer looking so depressed and ill.

Toscanini did not realise just how ill Puccini was. In fact, the composer had first begun to complain about a sore throat and persistent cough at the beginning of the year. However, he had always had a cough as he was a very heavy smoker. By March, he consulted his local doctor and a Milanese specialist, who suggested it was rheumatic inflammation that might benefit from some treatment at the health resort of Salsomaggiore near Parma. But, on 1 June, he told Sybil that his throat was just the same and the cure did not seem to have made any difference.

174

From left to right Renato Simoni, Puccini and Giuseppe Adami.

'They say I shall be better later – we'll see.' Exactly three months later, he indicated much more concern to Adami, though he had been reassured by the doctors: 'I am starting writing letters again. I have been passing through tremendous crises – also with regard to my health. That trouble in my throat, which has tormented me since March, seemed a grave matter. I feel better now, and also have the assurance that it is rheumatic in origin and that, with treatment, it will improve. But I have had some very sad days.'

In fact, Sybil Seligman had visited him in August, and had suspected that the diagnosis might be incorrect. Alerted by her, Tonio urged his father to consult another doctor, but Giacomo kept delaying until the pain grew more intense in October. He first saw a specialist in Viareggio, and then another in Florence, who diagnosed a small tumour under the epiglottis. Giacomo seems not to have realised the full implications of this, but Tonio contacted the the throat specialist without his father's knowledge, and was told that his father had advanced and inoperable cancer of the throat. Tonio arranged a further consultation with three more specialists, who confirmed the diagnosis, but suggested that the only hope lay in treatment by X-ray. This branch of medicine was still in its early stages, so it was decided that Giacomo should go to one of the few clinics that were properly equipped, the Brussels Institut de la Couronne, the director of which was a Dr Ledoux.

Before going, Puccini consulted with Toscanini again about

175

the first production of *Turandot*, though the conductor had been warned by Tonio about the seriousness of the illness. Puccini still seemed unaware of the possible implications, as did Elvira, who did not accompany her husband to Brussels owing to a bad bout of bronchitis. He set out on 4 November, accompanied by Tonio, taking with him 36 pages of *Turandot* – the sketches for the love duet and the finale, the only sections still unfinished. He would never complete them. While the initial stage of treatment by X-ray was in progress, he was allowed to leave the clinic, and so he was able to see what turned out to be the last performance he would hear of one of his operas – *Madama Butterfly* at the Théâtre de la Monnaie.

While in Brussels, he wrote several times to a friend and hunting companion in Viareggio, Angiolino Magrini. 'I am in the hands of the doctors and of God,' he said in his first letter, while a later one gave a graphic account of the treatment:

I am crucified like Christ! I have a collar round my throat, which is absolute torture. For the moment, the X-ray treatment is external, later crystal needles into my neck and a hole in order to breathe, this too in my neck. But don't mention this to Elvira or anyone else.

The thought of that hole, with a rubber or silver tube in it – I don't know what – terrifies me. They say I won't suffer at all and I must just put up with it for eight days, so as not to disturb the part that has to be healed. To breathe in the normal way would irritate it. So I will have to breathe through a tube! My God, what a horror!...

What a calamity! May God help me. It will be a long treatment – six weeks – and terrible. However, they assure me I shall be cured. I am a little sceptical about it, and am prepared for anything. I'm thinking of my family, of poor Elvira. From the day of my departure, my disease has grown worse. I spit mouthfuls of black blood in the mornings. But the doctor says that is nothing and I must be calm now that the cure has begun. We shall see, dear Angiolino.

Clausetti, as the representative of Ricordi, had already arrived in Brussels, and on Saturday 22 November Tonio summoned his sister, Fosca, and Magrini, since the operation was to be carried out on the Monday. They were joined in Brussels by Toscanini's wife, Carla. Elvira was confined to Milan, still not aware of the true nature of her husband's illness. The operation to insert seven needles round the tumour was done under local anaesthetic, because of concern about the patient's heart. It lasted nearly four hours. Dr Ledoux was satisfied and there was room for some optimism over the next three days. In great pain, fed through a tube in his nose, unable to speak, the composer communicated by gestures and written notes. 'I seem to have bayonets in my

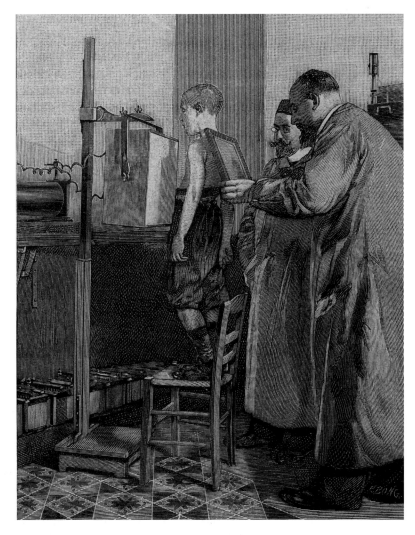

throat; they have massacred me,' he wrote at one point. Clausetti wrote to Adami: 'Things are going better than anyone could have hoped. The doctors are now saying without any hesitation that Puccini will certainly be saved.' Dr Ledoux felt able to tell the directors of the Théâtre de la Monnaie: *Puccini en sortira* (Puccini will be coming out). On 28 November, the family were sufficiently confident to have lunch together in a nearby hotel, and Elvira sent a telegram of joy at the better news. At 4pm, Fosca sat down to write to her mother:

Everything is going well and the doctors are more than satisfied: our adored Papà is saved! *Saved* – do you understand? Certainly he has suffered a good deal, but from now on this terrible part of the cure is over, and he will only have to submit to the boredom of convalescence. There is no more physical suffering, and far less mental

177

suffering; it is only his nerves which have been upset, so the doctors tell us, by the radium which is at work.

That letter was never sent. At 6pm, Puccini collapsed in his chair from heart failure. Though the needles were removed, a night of terrible suffering followed. The Italian Ambassador and the Papal Nuncio called, the latter to give Puccini the last rites while he was still conscious. He died at 4am on 29 November 1924, three weeks short of his 66th birthday.

After a funeral service on 1 December in Brussels conducted by the Papal Nuncio, the body was taken to Milan by train for a service led by Cardinal Tosi in the Duomo, with Toscanini and the La Scala forces performing the Requiem from *Edgar*. A solemn procession escorted the coffin in pouring rain through the streets lined with thousands of mourners. The *cortège* stopped outside La Scala, which then remained closed as one of the many marks of national mourning in the days that followed. The body was given a temporary resting place in Toscanini's family tomb in Milan's Cimitero Monumentale. Two years later, Puccini was re-buried in the mausoleum Tonio had built in his beloved villa by the lake at Torre del Lago.

The composer's self-centredness in his life was reflected in his will, which left almost everything to Tonio and Elvira. He left nothing to the community, unlike Verdi, who had founded in his lifetime a Musicians' Rest Home and endowed it on his death. Many saw this as a measure of the difference in stature between the two men, the last giants of popular Italian opera.

Turandot was eventually completed by Franco Alfano, then 50, who had himself written seven operas. Toscanini had at first suggested Riccardo Zandonai, but Tonio felt he was too well known in his own right. It took Alfano six months to finish it, and, when he asked Toscanini for his opinion at the dress rehearsal, the conductor is said to have replied: 'I saw Puccini approaching from the rear of the stage to clout me.' The première was given at La Scala on 25 April 1926 with Rosa Raisa as Turandot, Miguel Fleta as Calaf, and Maria Zamboni as Liù. Mussolini, in Milan to celebrate Fascist Empire Day, was invited and accepted, asking that the Fascist hymn be played first. Toscanini refused, so Mussolini did not come. Puccini had prophesied that, if he did not complete the opera, 'someone will come to the front of the stage and say: "Puccini composed as far as this, then he died."' At the première Toscanini laid down his baton and said: 'The opera ends here; at this point Giacomo Puccini broke off his work. Death on this occasion was stronger than art.' On this night only the curtain came down at this point and the performance ended.

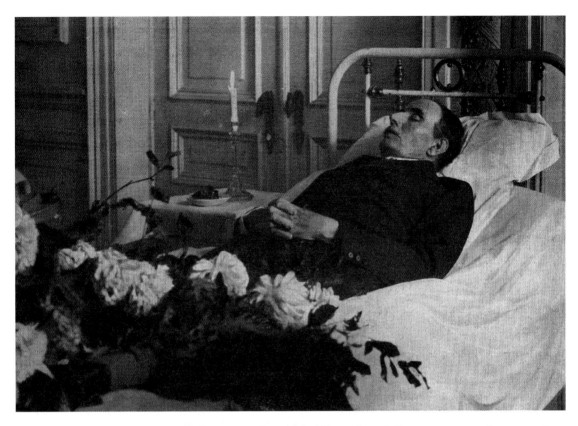

Puccini on his death-bed.

Gaetano Cesari in *Il corriere della sera* wrote the next day: 'How extraordinary is the power of evocation possessed by music which bears in itself the clear imprint of the composer's personality! Last night at La Scala, Puccini was with us. He was with the great public, who had admired and applauded him in the days of his most splendid triumphs.' Because it was, in part, not like the familiar Puccini of his most popular operas, *Turandot*, while being greeted enthusiastically and performed all over the world, has taken longer to achieve the full recognition it now justly enjoys.

To know and understand Puccini's life is to understand his music more deeply, for he was an instinctive composer whose feelings and experiences moulded his works; he described himself as a composer with 'more heart than mind'. Yet he reveals not only a great deal about himself, but also much for the perceptive listener. He deals, above all, with those passions that drive and inspire human beings, but which can also torment and destroy them. Many find it uncomfortable, or even painful, to face such exposed truth, such naked emotion, and such probing into the raw nerves of human existence. The critic who dismisses Puccini's middle period operas as lacking in intellectual depth should examine whether he or she has

179

Statue of Puccini erected
near his villa at Torre del
Lago.

other motives for not wishing to hear too closely what Puccini has to convey. In *Gianni Schicchi* and *Turandot*, there are signs of an advance in depth that have led many to question what he might have achieved if he had lived as long as Verdi or Wagner. Or does his inability to 'soar to the heights' with the love duet of Turandot and Calaf indicate that his undoubted creative gifts and his many moments of genius had their limits, which he intuitively knew he had reached?

Puccini's principal operas retain their prominent place in the world operatic repertoire mainly because of their moments of great theatre, because they evoke and touch profound emotions in those who hear and see them, and because they contain such inventive melody. 'Without melody, fresh and poignant,' Puccini once wrote, 'there can be no music.' His ability to create lyrical lines and phrases that convey so exactly the emotion of a character at a particular moment is surely his greatest gift. By his unique ability to blend music, words and dramatic action to create powerful dramas in music, he carried forward the glorious tradition of Italian opera he had inherited from his predecessors, Rossini, Bellini, Donizetti and Verdi. That great century of Italian operatic composition came to an end with his death. Yet through the music and the stories of his heroines (Manon, Mimi, Tosca, Butterfly and the rest), essentially flawed as human beings, yet vibrant with life, we can still touch, and be touched by, the exuberant and tragic spirit of the Maestro from Lucca.

Puccini's Works

Listed below are all of Puccini's operas. Librettists and sources are given, followed by details of first performances. Other minor works mentioned in the text, or of note, are also given.

Operas

Le villi (Ferdinando Fontana, after Alphonse Karr: *Les willis*)
  [Teatro dal Verme, Milan 31 May 1884; revised version: Teatro
  Regio, Turin 26 December 1884]

Edgar (Fontana, after Alfred de Musset: *La Coupe et les Lèvres*)
  [La Scala, Milan 21 April 1889; 2nd version: Teatro Communale,
  Ferrara 28 February 1892; final version: Buenos Aires Opera
  8 July 1905]

Manon Lescaut (Marco Praga, Domenico Oliva, Ruggero
  Leoncavallo, Luigi Illica and Giuseppe Giacosa, after Abbé
  Prévost: *L'Histoire du Chevalier des Grieux et de Manon Lescaut*)
  [Teatro Regio, Turin 1 February 1893]

La bohème (Illica and Giacosa, after Henri Mürger: *Scènes de la vie de
  bohème*)
  [Teatro Regio, Turin 1 February 1896]

Tosca (Illica and Giacosa, after Victorien Sardou: *La Tosca*)
  [Teatro Costanzi, Rome 14 January 1900]

Madama Butterfly (Illica and Giacosa, after David Belasco: *Madame
  Butterfly* based on a story by John Luther Long)
  [La Scala, Milan 17 February 1904; 2nd version: Teatro Grande,
  Brescia 28 May 1904; 3rd version: Covent Garden, London
  10 July 1905; 4th version (3 acts) Opéra-Comique, Paris 28
  December 1906]

La fanciulla del West (Guelfo Civinini and Carlo Zangarini, after
  David Belasco: *The Girl of the Golden West*)
  [Metropolitan Opera, New York 10 December 1910]

La rondine (Giuseppe Adami, after Alfred Willner and Heinz Reichert)
  [Monte Carlo Opera 27 March 1917]

Il trittico
  - *Il tabarro* (Adami, after Didier Gold: *La houppelande*)
  - *Suor Angelica* (Giovacchino Forzano)

- *Gianni Schicchi* (Forzano, after Dante: *Inferno, xxx*)
  [Metropolitan Opera, New York 14 December 1918]
Turandot (Adami and Renato Simoni, after Carlo Gozzi and
  Friedrich von Schiller)
  [La Scala, Milan 25 April 1926]

Chamber Music
String Quartet in D [between 1880 and 1883]
Fugues for string quartet [1882-3]
La Sconsolata for violin and piano [1883]
Crisantemi for string quartet [pub. 1890]

Choral Music
Cantata: *I figli d'Italia bella* [1877]
Cantata a Giove [1897]
Inno a Diana for chorus and piano (Carlo Abeniacar) [1897]
Inno di Roma [Rome, June 1919]

Church Music
Vexilla Regis (Venantius Honorius Fortunatus)
  [between 1874 and 1880]
Salve Regina (Antonio Ghislanzoni) [c.1882-3]
Mass for four voices and orchestra [1880]
Requiem for mixed voice and organ or harmonium [1905]

Orchestral Works
Preludio sinfonico [1876]
Capriccio sinfonico [1883]

Songs
'A Te' [a student work, author and date unknown]
'Ad una morta – Spirto gentil' (Antonio Ghislanzoni) [1882]
'Mentia l'avviso' (Felice Romani) [1883]
'Storiella d'amore' (Ghislanzoni) [1883]
'Sole e amore' (Puccini) [1883]
'Avanti, Urania!' (Renato Fucini) [1896]
'E l'uccellino' (Fucini) [1899]
'Terra e mare' (Enrico Panzacchi) [1902]
'Canto d'anime' (Illica) [1904]
'Morire?' (Adami) [1917]

Selected Bibliography

Adami, Giuseppe, ed.: *Letters of Puccini* trans. Eva Makin, revised
  and introduced by Mosco Carner, revised edn., London, 1974
Adami, Giuseppe: *Puccini* Milan, 1935
Ashbrook, William: *The Operas of Puccini* revised edn. Oxford, 1985
Budden, Julian: *Puccini, Giacomo* and entries on each opera in
The New Grove Dictionary of Opera ed. Stanley Sadie, in four volumes,
  London, 1992
Carner, Mosco: *Puccini: a Critical Biography* 2nd edn., London, 1974
  'Giacomo Puccini', *The New Grove Masters of Italian Opera*
  London, 1983
  Madama Butterfly London, 1979
  Giacomo Puccini: Tosca Cambridge, 1985
Casini, Claudio: *Giacomo Puccini* Turin, 1978
Di Gaetani, J.L.: *Puccini the Thinker: the Composer's Intellectual and
  Dramatic Development* New York, 1987
Dry, Wakeling: *Giacomo Puccini* London, 1906
Fiorentino, Dante del: *Immortal Bohemian: An Intimate Memoir of
  Giacomo Puccini* London, 1952
Fraccaroli, A.: *La vita di Giacomo Puccini* Milan, 1925
Gara, Eugenio, ed.: *Carteggi pucciniani* Milan, 1958
Girardi, M.: *Puccini: la vita e l'opere* Rome, 1989
Greenfeld, Howard: *Puccini: A Biography* London, 1981
Greenfield, Edward Harry: *Puccini: Keeper of the Seal*
  London, 1958
Groos, Arthur and Parker, Roger: *Giacomo Puccini: La bohème*
  Cambridge, 1986
Hughes, Spike: *Famous Puccini Operas* revised edn., New York, 1972
Jackson, Stanley: *Monsieur Butterfly: The Story of Puccini*
  London, 1974
Kaye, M.: *The Unknown Puccini* Oxford, 1985
Magri, G.: *Puccini e le sue rime* Milan, 1974
Marchetti, Arnaldo and Giuliani, Vittorio: *Puccini com'era*
  Milan, 1983
Marchetti, Leopoldo: *Puccini nelle immagini* revised edn., Rita Puccini,
  Milan, 1968

184

Marek, George: *Puccini* London, 1952

Marotti, G. and Pagni, F.: *Giacomo Puccini intimo* Florence, 1926

Marotti, G.: *Giacomo Puccini* Florence, 1949

Osborne, Charles: *The Complete Operas of Puccini: A Critical Guide* London, 1981

Paladini, C.: *Giacomo Puccini* Florence, 1961

Pintorno, G.: *Puccini: 276 lettere inedite* Montecatini, 1974

Puccini, S. ed.: *Giacomo Puccini: lettere a Riccardo Schnabel* Milan, 1981

Ricci, L.: *Puccini interprete di se stesso* Milan, 1954

Sartori, C.: *Puccini* 4th edn., Milan, 1978

Seligman, Vincent: *Puccini among Friends* London, 1938

Specht, Richard: *Giacomo Puccini: The Man, His Life, His Work* trans. Catherine Phillips, London, 1933

Torrefranca, Fausto: *Giacomo Puccini e l'opera internazionale* Turin, 1912

Weaver, William: *Puccini: the Man and his Music* London, 1978

Acknowledgements and References

Acknowledgements are due for quotations from the following sources:

G. Adami (ed.) (rev.M.Carner), *Letters of Puccini* (London, Harrap, 1974); M. Carner, *Puccini* (London, Duckworth, 1974); W. Dry, *Giacomo Puccini* (London, Bodley Head,1906);H. Greenfeld, *Puccini* (London, 1980); G. Hall, *Sleeve note to Puccini's Suor Angelica* (London, Decca); H.Klein, *The Golden Age of Opera* (London, Routledge, 1933); G. Marek *Puccini: A Biography* (London, Cassell, 1952); C. Osborne, *The Complete Operas of Puccini: a critical guide* (London, Gollancz, 1981); C. Osborne, *Letters of Giuseppe Verdi* (London, Cassell, 1971); Rosenthal and Warrack, *The Concise Oxford Dictionary of Opera* (2nd edn.) (OUP, 1973); S. Sadie (ed.), *The New Grove Dictionary of Opera* (London, Macmillan Publishers Limited, 1992); V. Seligman, *Puccini Among Friends* (London, Macmillan, 1938).

Every effort has been made to trace copyright holders for the illustrative material used in the book. Apologies are extended to those whom it has not been possible to contact.

Picture credits
Hulton Deutsch 22, 25, 31, 41, 57, 61, 67, 69, 74, 75, 78, 93, 94, 97, 99, 106, 110, 121, 130, 133, 180

Mary Evans Picture Library 6, 11, 13, 15, 18, 20, 21, 23, 24, 30, 33, 34, 36, 37, 39, 43, 45, 47, 48, 49, 55, 60, 65, 66, 71, 72, 73, 77, 80, 82, 86, 88, 90, 91, 100, 101, 109, 111, 113, 118, 120, 128, 131, 132, 135, 137, 138, 147, 150, 152, 154, 156, 157, 159, 160, 168, 169, 171, 175, 177, 179

National Gallery of Art, Washington 68

Royal Opera House, Covent Garden 89, 111, 123

Museo di Torre del Lago Puccini

186

Index

*Page numbers in **bold** refer to illustrations*

187